MODERN STUDIES
DEMOCRACY IN SCOTLAND AND THE UK

D0714556

Frank Cooney, Gary Hughes
and David Sheerin

HODDER
GIBSON
AN HACHETTE UK COMPANY

The Publishers would like to thank the following for permission to reproduce copyright material:

Photo credits

p.2 ©WPA Pool/Pool/GettyImages; p.5 © Dan Kitwood/Getty Images; p.7 © Sergio Azenha/Alamy Stock Photo; p.8 (top) © rnl – Fotolia, (bottom) © Eain Scott/istockphoto; p.9 © johnboy – Fotolia; p.14 © Mirrorme22/https://commons.wikimedia.org/wiki/File:United_Kingdom_EU_referendum_2016_area_results_2-tone.svg/https://creativecommons.org/licenses/by-sa/3.0/deed.en; p.16 © idp navy collection/Alamy Stock Photo; p.18 (top) © epa european pressphoto agency b.v./Alamy Stock Photo, (bottom) © Yes Scotland; p.19 © Better Together 2012 Limited; p.20 © epa european pressphoto agency b.v./Alamy Stock Photo; p.24 © BEN STANSALL/AFP/Getty Images; p.28 © Guy Corbishley/Alamy Stock Photo; p.30 © Gareth Fuller/PA Archive/Press Association Images; p.47 (left) © C Squared Studios/Photodisc/Getty Images/ European Objects OS44, (right) © Tyler Olson - SimpleFoto/Fotolia; p.54 © mark severn/Alamy Stock Photo; p.57 © Ken McKay/ITV/REX/Shutterstock; p.65 © Roger Gaisford/Alamy Stock Photo; p.72 © Ken Jack/Alamy Stock Photo; p.76 © Ken Jack/Alamy Stock Photo; p.77 © Ken Jack/Corbis/Getty Images; p.80 © Russell Hart/Alamy Stock Photo; p.82 © Permission cleared from COSLA (http://www.cosla.gov.uk/); p.86 (top) © LESLEY MARTIN/AFP/Getty Images, (bottom) © Art Conaghan/Photoshot; p.93 © AP/Press Association Images; p.95 © PA Wire / PA Archive/Press Association Images; p.98 © PA / PA Archive/Press Association Images; p.105 (left) © REX/Shutterstock, (right) © BEN STANSALL/Getty Images; p.106 © epa european pressphoto agency b.v./Alamy Stock Photo; p.115 © Guy Corbishley/Alamy Stock Photo; p.118 © Craig Redmond/Alamy Stock Photo; p.120 © Steven Scott Taylor/Alamy Stock Photo; p.123 © Michael Kemp/Alamy Stock Photo; p.125 © keith morris news/Alamy Stock Photo; p.129 © Karwai Tang/WireImage/Getty Images; p.130 © Matt Crossick / Matt Crossick/Empics Entertainment; p.133 © Twitter; p.135 © David Sheerin; p.138 © David Sheerin.

Chapter opener image reproduced on pages 1, 15, 28, 46, 60, 85, 114, 126 and 135 © Claudio Divizia – Fotolia.

Orders: please contact Bookpoint Ltd, 130 Park Drive, Milton Park, Abingdon, Oxon OX14 4SE. Telephone: (44) 01235 827720. Fax: (44) 01235 400454. Lines are open 9.00–5.00, Monday to Saturday, with a 24-hour message answering service. Visit our website at www.hoddereducation.co.uk. Hodder Gibson can be contacted direct on: Tel: 0141 333 4650; Fax: 0141 404 8188; email: hoddergibson@hodder.co.uk.

© Frank Cooney, Gary Hughes and David Sheerin 2016

First published in 2016 by
Hodder Gibson, an imprint of Hodder Education,
An Hachette UK Company
211 St Vincent Street
Glasgow G2 5QY

Impression number   5 4 3 2 1

Year   2020 2019 2018 2017 2016

Cover photo Scottish Parliament/https://creativecommons.org/licenses/by/2.0
Illustrations by Integra Software Services Pvt., Ltd.
Typeset in Minion/Regular 12/15 by Integra Software Services Pvt., Ltd.
Printed in Slovenia

A catalogue record for this title is available from the British Library

ISBN: 978 1 4718 3589 6

Contents

1 The UK constitutional arrangements

The structure of the government

The United Kingdom is a parliamentary democracy with a constitutional monarch as head of state. The present monarch, the Queen, has no political power, and the royal prerogatives are exercised by the prime minister and government ministers, who in turn are responsible to an elected House of Commons (see box The constitutional monarchy). While Americans might refer to the monarch as Queen of England, she is queen to the people of England, Northern Ireland, Scotland and Wales and to the people of the 15 realms of the Commonwealth.

In the United Kingdom all powers are invested in the UK Parliament and this is referred to as parliamentary sovereignty. However, present membership of the European Union (EU) and acceptance of the European Convention of Human Rights (ECHR) have diminished parliamentary sovereignty. The new Conservative Government as part of its election manifesto is considering abolishing the Human Rights Act and replacing it with a British Bill of Rights (see pages 4–5). The Conservative Government held a referendum on the UK remaining within the EU in June 2016 (see pages 9–14).

The constitutional monarchy

Prerogative functions

The British monarch retains some longstanding common law powers known as royal prerogatives. The present monarch, Queen Elizabeth, became Queen in 1952 and is the longest serving monarch. The royal family plays a very visible part in British politics even though these powers are exercised by the prime minister. The Queen and Prince Charles are routinely informed about policy decision making and have access to confidential papers. Prince Charles, for example, sends numerous letters to government ministers outlining his views.

Opening Parliament

The parliamentary year runs from the date when the monarch 'summons' (opens) Parliament until the date when it is 'prorogued' (closed). The monarch reads out the government's major policy proposals, which is currently referred to as the 'Queen's speech'.

Dissolution of Parliament

The maximum term of any parliament is five years, at the end of which the monarch declares that the parliament is dissolved. Prior to the Parliament of 2010–15, the prime minister could use this power to dissolve parliament at any point during the five years. However, the UK now has fixed-term parliaments.

Appointing the prime minister and first minister

The monarch still 'appoints' all Ministers of the Crown including the executive heads of government. By convention the leader of the largest party is usually invited to form a government. This government is referred to as 'Her/His Majesty's Government'.

The royal assent

A bill that has passed through the required legislative process in the Houses of Parliament and devolved assemblies must receive the royal assent from the monarch before it becomes law.

Symbolic functions

Head of State

It is the monarch rather than the prime minister who is head of state. In the USA the president is head of state.

Head of the Commonwealth

The monarch is the head of the 'Family of Nations' and usually opens Commonwealth Conferences.

Figure 1.1 **The Queen opening Parliament**

The British Constitution

A constitution is a set of rules that lays down the powers and duties of the institutions of government and establishes the rights and liberties of citizens.

Unlike all other major states the UK does not have a written constitution. Critics argue that this is a major flaw in our democratic structure. We may have conventions and statute law, but a government with a majority is often described as an 'elected dictatorship' with little effective scrutiny from parliament. In contrast, the US Constitution limits the power of the Executive through the separation of powers between the different branches of government. An American president envies the powers of a UK prime minister.

No UK party has won a general election with more than 50 per cent of the vote since 1935, yet the winning party usually wins a majority of seats in the House of Commons. This enables the government to use this majority to govern as it wishes with limited checks to its powers. This is described as an elected dictatorship as the Legislature cannot check the actions of the Executive (the opposite of the American system). As an example of this, in 2003 Prime Minister Blair went to war against Iraq without consulting Parliament.

The UK's constitutional arrangements are uncodified which means that the rules that govern our country can be amended relatively easily through parliamentary statutes (laws such as the 2011 Fixed-term Parliament Act – see page 3). Further, many of the parliamentary procedures and constitutional principles are based not on laws but on 'convention' (see page 3). Important conventions such as collective Cabinet responsibility have become established principles and practice of Cabinet government.

Parliamentary democracy

The Executive part of government is drawn from the Legislature and is, in turn, accountable to it.

Royal prerogative

Powers of the monarch that are exercised in the crown's name by the prime minister and government ministers.

Devolved

Powers that have been transferred from central government to local or regional administration.

Referendum

The electorate, not their representatives, vote to accept or reject a proposal.

2011 Fixed-term Parliament Act

This Act is an example of how a previous unwritten part of the constitution can be replaced by a codified statute. Prior to this Act the convention was that the prime minister, using the royal prerogative power of dissolution, had the right to decide when a general election would be held during the parliament's five-year term.

Now under the above Act a general election was held on the first Thursday in May 2015 and, if not repealed, the subsequent election will be held in May 2020.

Examples of constitutional conventions

- The House of Lords does not oppose legislation contained within the government's manifesto (the Salisbury Convention). However, the Liberal Democrat peers rejected this government mandate in 2005. They argued that the Labour Government had been elected by only 35 per cent of the vote and the Liberal Democrat peers voted against the introduction of identity cards, a policy within the Labour election manifesto (see also House of Lords' opposition to welfare cuts, page 98).
- The prime minister is the leader of the largest party – or coalition of parties – in the House of Commons.
- Money bills are the responsibility of the House of Commons.
- The monarch grants royal assent to all parliamentary legislation.
- Individual ministerial responsibility requires a minister to resign following significant departmental failure.

Constitutional conventions that are now codified

The Sewel Convention established that Westminster would not legislate on matters affecting devolved administrations without their consent. In 2005 this convention was codified and enshrined within Parliament's Standing Orders as Legislative Consent Motions.

The convention that the prime minister chooses the date of an election (within a five-year period) was ended by the 2011 Fixed-term Parliament Act (see box above).

Should the UK have a written (codified) constitution?

No

1 Our uncodified constitution provides flexibility.

It can adapt to changing circumstances and to political pressure. An excellent example is the creation of the Scottish Parliament and the granting of further powers to the Scottish Government. The UK Constitution has adapted to EU membership and reform of the House of Lords, which further highlights its flexibility.

2 As implied, it is easy to change and it works.

There are no cumbersome arrangements to change the constitution, unlike in the USA. It can be changed by a simple Act of Parliament. The present system has been continually tested and proved worthy.

3 It usually ensures strong and accountable government. In the UK model, there is no conflict between the Executive and the Legislature. Contrast this with the US and the failure of President Obama to pass key legislation through a hostile Republican-controlled Congress.

4 Parliamentary sovereignty is at the centre of our constitution and this enables a party with a majority in the House of Commons to deliver its election manifesto. Both Margaret Thatcher and Tony Blair introduced significant political, social and economic change to Britain. Contrast this with President Obama's failure to achieve new gun control laws.

Yes

1 A written constitution provides clarity.

It is usually contained in one single document and is clear and accessible to all citizens. It is easy to understand and everyone can refer to it when necessary. Its lack of ambiguity should reduce the possibility of political disputes.

2 It provides limited government and in theory should encourage consensus government.

3 A written constitution within a democracy prevents the Executive becoming too powerful. The US Constitution enshrines the separation of powers between Executive, Legislature and Judiciary to ensure that the president does not become a dictator. In contrast, the UK Executive has been called an elected dictatorship, whereby a government elected with only a minority of the popular vote can make profound changes to the UK Constitution, for example the attempt by Labour in 2006 to bring in identity cards.

4 It protects human rights.

A written constitution guarantees the rights of its citizens through a document referred to as the Bill of Rights. This document is enshrined within the constitution. This can prevent the state abusing its powers under the cloak of national security.

Abolition of the Human Rights Act

The Conservatives' manifesto in 2015 stated that the party would scrap the Human Rights Act which had been passed in 1998 by the Labour Government. In practice, the Act has two main effects. Firstly, it incorporates the rights of the European Convention on Human Rights (ECHR) into domestic British law. What this means is that if someone has a complaint under human rights law they do not have to go to European courts but can get justice from British courts. Secondly, it requires all public bodies – not just the central government, but institutions like the police, National Health Service (NHS) and local councils – to abide by these human rights.

It should be pointed out that the European Convention on Human Rights has nothing to do with the European Union and predates it by decades. Its institutions and courts are completely separate. Ratification of the convention is a condition of being a member of the European Union. (Every European country except Belarus – Europe's last military dictatorship – is a member of the European Convention on Human Rights.)

The Conservatives would replace it with what they call a 'British Bill of Rights'. They argue this new bill will 'break the formal link between British Courts and the European Court of Human Rights'. In practice, this would likely mean that people who wanted to bring human rights cases under the ECHR would have to go to a court in Strasbourg to be heard.

The Scottish Government has strongly opposed any move to abolish the Human Rights Act. In the face of strong opposition the Conservative Government has delayed any repeal and has set up a working group to reconsider the issue.

The UK Judiciary

One hallmark of a democracy is the existence of an independent judiciary and over the last few decades judicial independence in the UK has been strengthened

Actions to strengthen the Judiciary

- The Constitutional Reform Act 2005 set up the independent Supreme Court as the highest court in the UK. To further ensure judicial independence, the Lord Chancellor is no longer the head of the Judiciary. This ensures that government ministers are barred from trying to influence judicial decisions through direct access to judges.
- Judges are being increasingly appointed by the Judicial Appointments Commission rather than by the government. However, the prime minister can exercise their power to veto appointments.
- Judges of the High Court and above can only be dismissed by both Houses of Parliament.

Figure 1.2 **British Supreme Court judges**

Conflict between Judiciary and Executive

With the threat from international terrorism there can be tension between protecting the rights of citizens and maintaining state security. Successive governments have been unhappy that judges have opposed executive action, citing the Human Rights Act. On numerous occasions the then Home Secretary Theresa May has criticised the legal decisions of judges. For example, many foreign criminals have avoided government deportation orders by citing Human Rights Act Article 8 'Right to a family life' (see pages 112–13).

Show your understanding

1 Outline the prerogative powers of the monarchy.
2 Give three examples of constitutional conventions.
3 Outline the arguments for and against a written constitution.
4 In what ways has the judicial independence of the Judiciary been strengthened in recent years?
5 Why is there opposition to the Conservatives' pledge to abolish the Human Rights Act?

Research activity

Should the UK have a written constitution? Working in pairs, investigate this issue and present your findings to the class.

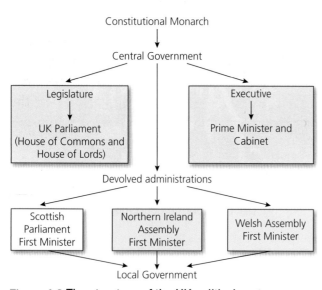

Figure 1.3 **The structure of the UK political system**

The role and powers of the devolved bodies

We now have devolved parliaments (assemblies) in Northern Ireland, Scotland and Wales which can pass laws linked to their devolved powers. All these laws must receive the royal assent from the Queen as advised by the prime minister. However, the powers devolved to the three

parliaments can be returned to the UK Parliament and the devolved parliaments dissolved. (The SNP proposed that the new Scotland Act 2015 should recognise the permanence of the Scottish Parliament – it was blocked by English Conservative MPs.)

The UK Central Government has responsibility for national affairs such as immigration, defence, foreign policy and the environment. In the UK, the prime minister leads the government with the support of the Cabinet and ministers. Departments and their agencies are responsible for putting government policy into practice.

In Northern Ireland, Scotland and Wales, some government policies and public services are different from those in England. The UK Central Government has given certain powers to devolved governments, so that they can make decisions for their own areas. The arrangements are different for each, reflecting their history and administrative structures.

Welsh Assembly

The National Assembly for Wales is the representative body, with law-making powers on devolved matters. It debates and approves legislation. The role of the Assembly is to scrutinise and monitor the Welsh Assembly Government. It has 60 elected members and meets in the Senedd.

Northern Ireland Assembly

The Northern Ireland Assembly was established as part of the Belfast Agreement (also known as the Good Friday Agreement) in 1998. Devolution to Northern Ireland was suspended in October 2002 and restored on 8 May 2007.

Scottish Parliament

The Scottish Parliament held its first election in 1999 and a coalition government of Labour and Liberal Democrats was set up (see Table 2.1, page 15). The Scottish Parliament debates topical issues and passes laws on devolved matters affecting Scotland. It also scrutinises the work and policies of the Scottish Government. It is made up of 129 elected Members of the Scottish Parliament (MSPs), and meets at Holyrood in Edinburgh. Its devolved powers such as education are listed in Table 1.1. However, more powers continued to be devolved to Scotland. As part

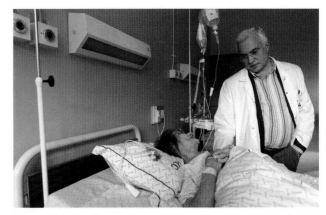

Figure 1.4 **The Scottish Government is responsible for health**

of the 2012 Scotland Act, MSPs at Holyrood are now responsible for laws on airguns and drink-driving limits (see page 16). During the 2014 Scottish Referendum campaign, the three main UK parties promised far greater powers to be granted to the Scottish Parliament. This was to persuade Scottish voters to remain within the UK. This promise of further powers – called devo-max – became the blueprint for the Scotland Act of 2015–16 (see pages 25–27).

Table 1.1 **Reserved and devolved powers of the Scottish Parliament (October 2015)**

Reserved issues include:	Scottish devolved powers include:
• Constitutional matters • UK foreign policy • UK defence and national security • Fiscal, economic and monetary system • Immigration and nationality • Energy: electricity, coal, gas and nuclear energy • Common markets • Trade and industry, including competition and customer protection • Some aspects of transport, including railways, transport safety and regulation • Employment legislation • Social security • Gambling and the National Lottery • Data protection • Human fertilisation, embryology and genetics • Equal opportunities	• Education and training • Health (control of abortion was added in 2015 as part of the Scotland Act) • Local government • Social work • Housing • Planning • Tourism, economic development and financial assistance to industry • Some aspects of transport, including the Scottish road network, bus policy and ports and harbours • Law and home affairs, including most aspects of criminal and civil law, the prosecution system and the courts • Police and Fire services • The environment • Natural and built heritage • Agriculture, forestry and fishing • Sport and the arts

Figure 1.5 **Westminster (top) and Holyrood**

citizens, the UK is being swamped by workers from Eastern Europe – taking British jobs and claiming the generous welfare benefits that the UK offers. Supporters argue that British citizens can attend European universities and work anywhere in the 27 countries that make up the EU. Workers from other EU states contribute to our economy, and Scotland with an ageing population benefits from an influx of young workers and their families.

Relationships with the European Union

The UK is subject to EU legislation. UK government ministers are involved in deciding this EU legislation and should not agree to proposals before parliament has examined them. However, many EU laws are decided by qualified majority vote (QMV) under which national governments are unable to veto measures they oppose.

The impact of EU membership on decision making in the UK

The result of the EU Referendum on 23 June 2016 was for the UK to leave the European Union. However, this will take between two and five years to implement and so this section is based on our present membership, as of July 2016.

The United Kingdom has been a member of the European Union since 1973 and over the years greater economic, social and political co-operation and integration has had a significant impact on decision making in the UK. Critics argue that the UK Parliament is no longer sovereign and that EU edicts must be implemented (see Relationships with the European Union right). Critics of the EU argue that, with the free movement of all European

What is parliament's role in Europe?

- Scrutinising EU draft legislation and other EU documents.
- Changing UK law to reflect agreed EU legislation and treaties.
- Holding the government to account on its EU policies and negotiating positions in the EU institutions.

The Commons European Scrutiny Committee

This committee considers all EU documents and reports its opinion on the legal and political importance of each one. The committee may request further information from the government or recommend the document for debate in a European Legislation Committee or in the Commons chamber.

The Lords European Union Select Committee

This committee also examines proposals for EU legislation and works closely with its Commons counterpart. The Lords look at fewer EU documents but carry out detailed reviews on subjects selected for their general importance.

2004–07 Another 12 countries, mostly from Eastern Europe, join to make 27 countries in the EU.

2013–16 Crisis in the 16 eurozone countries with Ireland, Portugal and especially Greece facing grave economic problems.

23 June 2016 UK public votes to leave the EU.

Membership of the EU has had significant impact on the major UK parties. Labour's initial suspicion of the EEC (the European Economic Community) has long passed and it is a firm supporter of the EU. In contrast membership of the EU has led to division and tension within the Conservative Party. These tensions have been intensified with the rise of UKIP – the anti-EU party. In the 2014 European election UKIP won the most votes and seats. This led to many Conservative MPs demanding David Cameron take a hard line on Europe.

Figure 1.6 **The European Parliament**

History of the European Union

1951 The European Coal and Steel Community is set up by the six founding members.

1957 The Treaty of Rome introduces a common market for other goods.

1968 All European Economic Community (EEC) countries establish the same custom tariffs on goods from non-EEC countries.

1973 The EEC expands to nine members when the UK, Ireland and Denmark join.

1979 The first direct elections to the European Parliament are held.

1993 The single market is completed and the Treaty of Maastricht establishes the European Union (EU).

2002 Euro notes and coins are introduced. The UK refuses to join the eurozone.

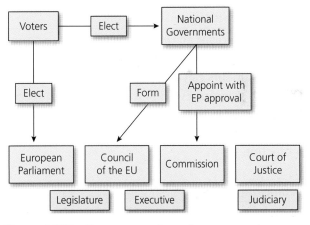

Figure 1.7 **The European system of government**

Why hold a referendum?

David Cameron made this promise in 2013 to placate the Eurosceptics within his party (81 Conservative MPs had defied a three-line whip to support an in–out referendum in October 2011, referred to as BREXIT). The success of UKIP in the 2014 European election and the defection of some Conservative MPs to UKIP confirmed the

Table 1.2 **Factors for and against the UK remaining in the EU**

The UK should remain in the EU	The UK should leave the EU
Political benefits	*Political factors and sovereignty*
The UK may have given up some national powers as a member of the EU. However, we have gained a voice within the global power that is the EU. We have greater international standing reinforced by our permanent seat in the UN Security Council. We also can provide serious military support to resolve conflict situations. Our international standing would be weakened if we left the EU. The threat from international terrorism, economic recession and the African refugee crisis requires a united EU response.	The UK would gain back its national sovereignty and the UK Parliament and courts would not need to enforce EU Directives. The Westminster Parliament would once again have parliamentary sovereignty.
Economic benefits	*Economic alternative to EU membership*
The EU is the world's largest single market with a total GDP greater than that of the USA. The single market of over 500 million people with no custom duties or tariffs provides great opportunities for British businesses. The UK Government estimates that 3.5 million jobs are linked to the UK's trade with other member states. It is true that Norway and Switzerland, who are not members of the EU, have strong economic ties. However, Norway has had to adopt 6,000 EU legislative Acts – without any say in the creation of these Acts.	The UK is a member of the World Trade Organisation (WTO), which has trade agreements with over 50 countries. As such the UK can leave the EU and still continue to trade with partners such as Switzerland. Also the UK pays more into the EU than it receives – an estimated net contribution of £10 billion.
Individual benefits	*Eurozone economies are in crisis*
Membership gives all UK citizens the right to study, work, live and have their pension paid into any EU nation. Students can apply to and attend universities abroad. Numerous EU Directives ensure better consumer protection including compensation for airport delays. We now have cleaner beaches, safer food and better animal protection.	The eurozone is a financial disaster with numerous countries, especially Greece, in serious financial difficulties. The possibility of a Greek default on its debts remains a real threat. Such a default would weaken the UK economy. The rush to economic unity through the adoption of the euro has brought misery and unemployment to millions of EU citizens.
Democratic deficit?	*Democratic deficit?*
The decision-making process within the EU is said to lack accountability and as such there is a democratic deficit within the EU. However, the influence of the European Parliament has increased in recent years and it should not be forgotten that decisions made by the unelected Council of Ministers are decisions made by ministers from elected governments including Britain.	Decisions that impact on British citizens are made by faceless bureaucrats in Brussels and are destroying British values and traditions. British taxpayers are subsidising French and other European farmers. The EU is a 'gravy-train "for those who work in it"' – the total budget for EU administration is estimated at £34 billion per annum. The Common Fisheries Policy (CFP) has been a disaster for the Scottish fishing industry as the UK gave traditional UK fishing waters to the EU.

wisdom of this decision. It would be fair to say that Britain has always been rather half-hearted about the European Union. Britain joined the EEC (as it was then called) relatively late, and the Labour Government even held a referendum in 1975 on staying in or out: the UK public voted 60 per cent to remain in. The Conservative prime minister, Mrs Thatcher, had furious arguments with the EU to achieve a UK financial rebate in the 1980s and we have been reluctant to support further EU legislation. We declined to join the euro and as such are not in the EU inner circle.

The Conservative 2015 election manifesto stated that if the party won the election then it would try to negotiate a new agreement for the UK and hold a referendum on whether the UK should remain in the EU by 2017. Mr Cameron has tried to placate his Conservative anti-Europe MPs: in 2009 Conservative Euro MPs withdrew from the European People's Party, the umbrella organisation for the centre-right in the European Parliament. Again in 2011 the UK Parliament passed the 2011 European Union Act, which requires any further EU Treaty that transfers substantial new powers to the EU to be put to a British referendum. The referendum was held on 23 June 2016 (see pages 12–14).

Mr Cameron's reform demands

1   A stop to 'welfare tourism' by limiting some benefits for new immigrants. The UK Government wants a four-year ban on benefits being claimed by migrants who arrive from the rest of the EU.
2   A reduction in EU regulations.
3   The introduction of a British opt-out from the EU objective of 'even closer union among the peoples of Europe'.
4   The granting of greater powers to the national parliament to enable them to block EU legislation.
5   A guarantee that an increasingly integrated eurozone will not take action that is detrimental to non-eurozone EU members.

The Council of Ministers agreement, February 2016

The main points agreed are:

- **Eurozone**: Britain can stay out of the eurozone and retain the pound, without fear of discrimination. Any British money spent on bailing out eurozone nations will be reimbursed.
- **Child benefit**: Child benefit payments to migrant workers for children living overseas will be based on the rate paid in their home country.
- **Migrant welfare payments**: The UK can decide to limit in-work benefits for EU migrants during their first four years in the UK. This 'emergency brake' can be applied in the event of 'exceptional' levels of migration, but must be released within seven years.
- **Protection for the City of London**: Safeguards for Britain's large financial services industry to prevent eurozone regulations being imposed on it.
- **Sovereignty**: There is an explicit commitment that the UK will not be part of an 'ever closer union' with other EU member states. This will be incorporated in an EU treaty change.
- **'Red card' for national parliaments**: It will be easier for governments to band together to block unwanted legislation. If 55 per cent of national EU parliaments object to a piece of EU legislation it may be changed.
- **Some limits on free movement**: Automatic free movement rights will be denied to nationals of a country outside the EU who marry an EU national, as part of measures to tackle 'sham' marriages. There are also new powers to exclude people believed to be a security risk – even if they have no previous convictions.

The EU Referendum, 23 June 2016

'Independence day' or 'doomsday'?

The referendum campaigns for both the 'Remain' and 'Leave' parties were criticised for their negativity. Even the SNP agreed with Brexit supporters that the UK government had waged a 'Project Fear' campaign on behalf of 'Remain', with George Osborne warning that a 'Leave' vote would lead to an emergency austerity budget.

The turnout on the day of 72 per cent was 6 per cent higher than the level in the May 2015 General Election. Supporters of the 'Remain' campaign went to sleep on Thursday 23 June confident that the UK would remain in Europe – the financial market had indicated thus. The view of the City was that the British public had seen through the half-truths of the 'Leave' campaign: the London bus with the distortion that we paid £350 million pounds every week to the EU; the statement that Turkey was about to join the EU and its 75 million citizens would 'swamp' British shores; and finally the UKIP poster with its 'racist' overtones. No one knew what the constitutional and economic impact of leaving Europe would be, but many political commentators had speculated that it could lead

to the destabilisation of Northern Ireland and the threat of a second Scottish independence referendum; the possible collapse of the pound; higher inflation and unemployment and above all economic uncertainty.

Yet the 'Remain' supporters – the majority of them young, educated Scots, Irish and Londoners – woke up on Friday morning to the new reality that the UK would be leaving the EU. UKIP leader, Nigel Farage triumphantly declared 23 June as 'independence day for England'. The 'Leave' message that Britain should 'take back control' of its own affairs from the EU was a very effective slogan. Boris Johnson and Michael Gove, leading Conservatives in support of a 'Leave' vote, looked stunned as they addressed the media on Friday morning.

The reason for their victory was simple – the key issue for many voters was not free trade but immigration. Voting turnout in the areas of England and Wales that had suffered deindustrialisation and the impact of the savage austerity cuts was high. One 'Leave' voter in the Labour-dominated north of England summed it up: 'I have never voted before – what's the point? My life in poverty will never change, but in the referendum I had a chance to lash out at the London establishment and make a difference'. The political and social fault line between England and Scotland had widened. The paradox of the English dispossessed voting 'No' was that they had perhaps ushered in a harsher right-wing Conservative government, embarking on further, tighter austerity measures.

David Cameron must surely regret his gamble to resolve the internal conflict in the Conservative Party by calling the EU Referendum. Most likely, he will be remembered as the prime minister who needlessly ended our EU membership and his action could possibly lead to the break-up of the United Kingdom.

Table 1.3 **June 2016 EU Referendum results across the UK (%)**

Nation/Region	Remain	Leave
UK	48.1	51.9
England	46.6	53.4
Northern Ireland	55.8	44.2
Scotland	62.0	38.0
Wales	47.5	52.5
Selected Regions of England		
West Midlands	40.7	59.3
Yorkshire/Humber	42.3	57.7
South East	48.2	51.8
London	59.9	40.1

Key results and immediate consequences

- All of Scotland's 32 councils voted to remain in the UK.
- Moray, with the fishing industry at its heart, had the slimmest 'Remain' majority – just 122 votes.
- Edinburgh had the strongest city vote for 'Remain' at 74.4 per cent.
- Only 56.6 per cent of Glasgow's electorate voted – the UK's lowest turnout.
- Gibraltar had the biggest vote for 'Remain' at 95.6 per cent, and the strongest turnout of 83.5 per cent.
- Only 27 per cent of young voters voted to leave, compared to 60 per cent of elderly voters.
- David Cameron announced he would resign as prime minister and that the Conservative party would not only choose their new leader but the next prime minister. The Conservative Party and the Cabinet were in crisis.
- Nicola Sturgeon would explore all options to keep Scotland in the EU, including the strong possibility of holding a second referendum on Scottish Independence. She stated: 'Scotland faces the prospect of being taken out of the EU against our will. I regard that as democratically unacceptable.'

- Sinn Féin called for border poll on Irish unity as a consequence of the Brexit win. Inhabitants of Northern Ireland and the Republic of Ireland have the right to claim a passport from the Republic and thus remain EU citizens.
- The value of the pound plunged to a 30-year low and £50 billion was wiped off the share price of the UK's largest companies.
- EU leaders stated that it would not be 'an amicable divorce' and that the UK should immediately invoke Article 50 of the Lisbon Treaty and begin the formal process of leaving the EU.
- Labour leader, Jeremy Corbyn, was heavily criticised for his lack of leadership during the referendum campaign and was blamed for Labour supporters voting 'Leave'. Lance Price, former media adviser to Tony Blair, stated that 'Corbyn showed about as much enthusiasm for the EU as a vegetarian selling hot dogs'. Corbyn lost the support of his MPs with over 80 per cent supporting a motion of no confidence. Corbyn refused to resign and as such a further Labour leadership election was announced.
- By Sunday evening, two days after the result was announced, three million people had signed an online petition to hold a second EU referendum.
- Theresa May won the Conservative leadership election and became the new prime minister. She is only the second ever woman prime minister.

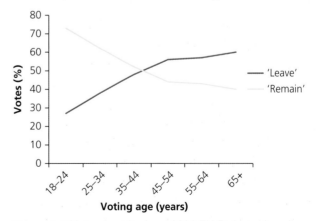

Figure 1.8 **Votes cast in June 2016 EU Referendum by voting age**
Source: Lord Ashcroft Poll

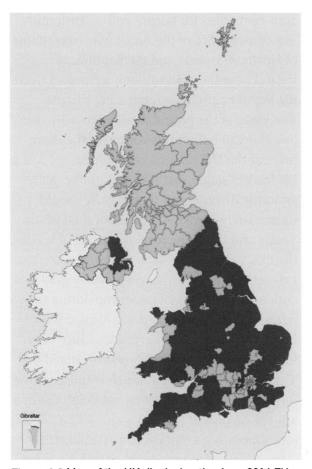

Figure 1.9 **Map of the UK displaying the June 2016 EU Referendum results (blue = 'Leave'; yellow = 'Remain')**
Source: Wikimedia Commons

Newspaper headlines and comments

Sunday Herald: '"English independence day" was fuelled by victimhood and muddled xenophobia'

The Times: 'Brexit earthquake'

Daily Star: 'Now let's make Britain great again'

Daily Express: 'World's most successive newspaper crusade ends in victory: we are out of Europe'

Sunday Mail: 'Defiant First Minister comes out fighting: we're going nowhere'

The Observer: 'UK faces a Brexit crisis as Europe's leaders demand: "Get out now!"'

The Economist: 'A tragic split'

Show your understanding

1 Describe the structure of the UK political system. (You should refer to the UK political system and devolved administrations.)
2 Outline the main devolved powers of the Scottish Government in the period 1999–2015.
3 Outline the impact of EU membership on UK Government decision making.
4 Outline the arguments for and against the UK remaining in the EU.
5 Outline the impact of the outcome of the June 2016 EU Referendum.

Added Value idea

Organise a class debate on the motion:
Leaving the EU will make the UK 'great again'.

2 Scotland and its constitutional future

Background

In 1979 the people of Scotland voted in a referendum on the setting up of a Scottish Assembly. Although there was a narrow victory for the 'Yes' vote, it failed to achieve the artificial threshold of 40 per cent of the electorate voting 'Yes'; and so no Scottish Assembly was set up.

From 1979 to 1997 the Conservative Party was in power in the UK and introduced policies that were unpopular in Scotland. It also rejected any form of devolution for Scotland. However, in 1997 the new Labour Government led by Tony Blair held a referendum to ask the Scottish people if they wanted a Scottish Parliament. And so in September 1997 the outcome of the referendum was a resounding 'Yes', with more than 74 per cent voting for the setting up of a Scottish Parliament.

The Scottish Parliament

In 1999 the Scottish Parliament came into being, and usually every four years we elect 129 MSPs and a Scottish Government to be responsible for the devolved powers given by the UK Parliament. However, since 2007 the SNP has formed the Scottish Government with a platform of greater powers for the Scottish Parliament (see Table 2.1).

All three Unionist parties – Labour, Conservative and Liberal Democrats – are against independence for Scotland. However, Labour, Liberal Democrats and Conservatives support greater powers being granted to the Scottish Parliament (albeit with slightly different versions). This is referred to as devo-max.

Table 2.1 **Elections and governments of Scotland 1999–2016**

Election	Government formed
1999	Labour and Liberal Democrats Coalition
2003	Labour and Liberal Democrats
2007	SNP Minority
2011	SNP Majority
2016	SNP Minority

The Calman Commission 2007–9

This Commission was set up in December 2007 to recommend any changes to the Scotland Act of 1998 that would enhance the role of the Scottish Parliament. It published its final report in June 2009.

The Scotland Act 2012

As a result of the Calman Report, and consensus among all of the UK parties, the UK Coalition Government granted further devolved powers to Scotland. The Scotland Act 2012 granted the Scottish Parliament greater taxation and borrowing powers and limited legislative powers over drugs, driving and guns.

2012 Scotland Act: Key measures

Income tax

From April 2016 half of the income tax paid by most Scots with their main residence in Scotland can be set by MSPs in Holyrood. They can set a new Scottish rate at 10p in the pound (meaning Scottish taxpayers will pay the UK rate) or vote to set the level higher or lower. In February 2016, the Scottish Government rejected Labour's proposal to raise income tax by 1 per cent for all taxpayers.

Full devolution of stamp duty and landfill tax

The Scottish Government can set the tax for stamp duty and landfill.

New borrowing powers

The Scottish Parliament is able to borrow up to £2.2 billion. Scotland used a limited version of this power to fund £100 million of pre-payment for the new Forth Road Crossing.

Power over airguns

Scottish ministers have introduced measures to ensure anyone who owns an airgun will need a licence and a legitimate reason to hold the weapon.

Drink-driving limits

Scotland used this new power to reduce the drink-driving limit from 80 mg to 50 mg per 100 ml of blood. This Act came into force in December 2014.

However, to the surprise and dismay of all the unionist parties, the SNP won the 2011 election by a landslide (the Additional Member System (AMS) of voting had been designed to prevent the SNP winning a majority).

With a clear mandate from the Scottish people, the SNP began negotiations to hold another referendum on Scottish independence with the Westminster Government. Finally in October 2012 both David Cameron and Alex Salmond signed the Edinburgh Agreement. The referendum would be held before the end of 2014 and the voting age would be reduced to 16.

Figure 2.1 **The UK's Trident nuclear deterrent is based at Faslane on the Clyde**

The Scottish Referendum, 18 September 2014

On 18 September 2014, the people of Scotland voted in a referendum on the constitutional future of Scotland. In a campaign that lasted for 30 months the people of Scotland were energised by the debate and the voters engaged in the discussion around the referendum question.

The question asked, to which voters were required to vote either 'Yes' or 'No', was: *Should Scotland be an independent country?*

Key points for and against independence in the 2014 Scottish Referendum

For

Defence The Yes Scotland campaign argued that an independent Scotland would be a member of NATO but without nuclear weapons. Trident nuclear submarines would be removed from Scotland.

NHS The SNP highlighted the further privatisation plans of the UK Government and claimed that the NHS was under threat. Sir Harry Burns, former Chief Medical Officer for Scotland, announced the week before the referendum that an independent Scotland was necessary to secure the future of the NHS.

Economy and oil Scotland has one of the highest GDPs (14th in the world) and has most of the EU's oil reserves and renewable energy. The present and future revenue from oil would ensure Scotland's economic viability and prosperity. An oil fund similar to that of Norway would be set up to protect Scotland if oil prices were to fall.

Currency It would be in the best interests of both an independent Scotland and the rest of the UK for Scotland to share the pound and retain the Bank of England as a lender of last resorts to bail out Scottish-based banks if needed. The economy of England would suffer if it excluded an independent Scotland from using the pound.

The European Union Scotland would not have to reapply to join the EU as citizens would continue to be EU citizens after a period of negotiation of Scotland's new terms.

National debt Scotland would honour its share of the national debt and would expect to retain the pound. It was not the English pound but the pound of all the nations of the UK.

Against

Defence The Better Together campaign argued that a nuclear-free Scotland would not be granted NATO membership. The removal of Trident would create significant job losses and damage Scotland's economy.

NHS Better Together also argued that as health is a devolved issue Scotland will always be able to protect the NHS from privatisation.

Economy and oil Opponents of Scottish independence argued that the Yes Scotland campaign overestimated the wealth that could be created by North Sea oil. The banking crisis of 2008–10 highlighted the need for Scotland to be part of a larger economy. Public spending in Scotland was £12,100 and for the UK it was £10,900 per head of population.

Currency The UK Coalition Government along with the Labour Party ruled out the possibility of a currency union with Scotland. Instead they suggested that Scotland would either have to use the pound in the same way that Panama uses the US dollar or set up a new currency or use the euro.

The European Union The UK Government argued that if Scotland voted to leave the UK it would have voted to leave an EU member state and would therefore have to reapply as a new member state relying on the support of governments such as Spain, who would not support such an application.

National debt Alistair Darling maintained that a currency union would not be possible in the event of independence and Scotland could not demand 'the best of both worlds'.

The road to the referendum

May 2011

The SNP won a majority in the Holyrood elections and the Scottish Parliament passed a historic and symbolic vote to hold a referendum on independence.

Figure 2.2 David Cameron and Alex Salmond signing the Edinburgh Agreement

October 2012: The Edinburgh Agreement

After months of tense negotiations, Scottish First Minister Alex Salmond and UK Prime Minister David Cameron signed an agreement to hold a one-question referendum by the end of 2014. The SNP persuaded the UK Government to change the electoral law to allow 16- and 17-year-olds to vote.

November 2013: White Paper on Independence

This 670-page White Paper sets out the case that an independent Scotland would have a strong economy and would be able to create a positive partnership with the remaining UK nations.

Independence White Paper

Below are some of its key statements:

- Scotland needs to tackle inequality both in wealth and health and can only achieve this by having complete control over pensions and welfare and the benefits system. The introduction of the bedroom tax and Universal Credit would be reversed.
- The NHS would remain in public hands and the privatisation of the NHS would be ended.
- Independence would make life better for Scots, and Scotland would take its place among member states of the EU and UN.
- Independence would address Scotland's 'democratic deficit' – 'for 34 out of 68 years since the Second World War, the nation has been governed by governments in Westminster that have no majority here'.
- It would be a modern, European democracy, founded on a written constitution with the Queen as Head of State.
- It would create a new Scottish Broadcasting Service (SBS) and Royal Mail would be brought back into public ownership.

The respective campaigns

Yes Scotland

YesScotland

In May 2012 Alex Salmond launched the campaign for independence and in terms of political parties Yes Scotland was supported by the SNP, the Scottish Greens and the Scottish Socialists. The general consensus was that the 'Yes' campaign had been enthusiastic, positive and people-centred. Yes Scotland, the umbrella group that orchestrated volunteers in 300 local groups, can take part of the credit for the highest ever level of voter registration in electoral history: 97 per cent and an 85 per cent turnout. Yes Scotland provided local campaigns with funds, merchandising and information. Their campaign was described as a 'festival of democracy'. New groups also emerged such as the left-wing Radical Independence Campaign which sent activists into Labour's stronghold housing estates. In one week in August 2014 this group door-stepped 18,000 voters in 90 working-class communities.

Better Together

bettertogether

In terms of political parties Better Together was supported by Labour, the Conservatives and the Liberal Democrats, with Alistair Darling (Labour) the leading figure. Its campaign to persuade the Scottish people to reject independence was launched in June 2012 by the Scottish leaders of these three unionist parties. Director of Better Together, Blair McDougall, a Labour Party national campaigner, concentrated on the uncertainties of independence and ran a negative campaign referred to as 'Project Fear' by the 'Yes' campaign. The Better Together campaign focused particularly around the future of Scotland's currency. Chancellor of the Exchequer George Osborne stated 'if Scotland walks away from the UK, it walks away from the UK pound'. Such a move would damage the Scottish economy and banking industry and the statement from the banks that they would have to move their headquarters to England frightened many Scots. There would be no amicable divorce. As political commentator Iain Macwhirter wrote, 'There was very little attempt by Better Together to offer a positive vision of a new progressive partnership between Scotland and England. It was a grudging "No" vote brought by threats and negativity.' For many Scots, especially the young, it seemed that the rest of the UK (rUK) would if necessary wreck

the Scottish economy rather than let Scotland create a mutually beneficial new economic partnership with rUK.

Show your understanding

1. Compare the types of government formed between 1999 and 2016.
2. Outline the devolved powers given to the Scottish Parliament by the Scotland Act 2012.
3. Outline the arguments for and against an independent Scotland.
4. Compare the campaign tactics of Yes Scotland and Better Together.

Result of the 2014 Scottish Independence referendum

The Scottish people voted to remain in the Union by a margin of 55 per cent to 45 per cent. A 'Yes' voter summed it up by saying: 'fear won over faith and greed over glory' (see voting analysis below). Opinion polls over the previous two decades had consistently stated that only 30 per cent of Scots wanted independence, yet a 'rogue' poll shortly before the referendum indicated that the 'Yes' vote had gained such momentum that it would achieve a majority result (in the weeks running up to elections the 'Yes' vote had increased to about 40 per cent). This created panic in Westminster with the leaders of the three major parties rushing north to support Gordon Brown's high profile campaign to persuade the Scots to reject independence. The three leaders issued the signed 'Vow' that the Scottish Parliament would receive more powers if independence was rejected (see *Daily Record* front page of 16 September 2014 – page 24).

Figure 2.3 Two Yes supporters draped in Scottish colours after the result

Turnout and patterns of voting

In all, 85 per cent of Scottish people turned out to vote in the referendum. In some regions, such as East Dunbartonshire and Stirling, turnout was over 90 per cent, the highest turnout ever recorded in a UK election or referendum (the lowest turnout was in Glasgow at 75 per cent). Four councils returned a majority 'Yes' vote – Dundee, Glasgow, North Lanarkshire and West Dunbartonshire – while the remaining 28 voted 'No'. This resulted in claims from many that the poorest in society had voted for change while in more affluent areas people were more likely to vote to remain part of the UK. It was also clear that a majority of the elderly and females voted 'No' (see Table 2.6).

However, it was widely acknowledged that even a 'No' vote was not a vote for the status quo and that the people of Scotland demanded change. Following the result Alex Salmond announced that he would stand down as party leader and as first minister. Nicola Sturgeon was elected party leader and became the first female first minister.

Table 2.2 **Results of the referendum: Should Scotland be an independent country?**

	Votes	**%**
Yes	1,617,989	44.7
No	2,001,926	55.3

Table 2.3 **Turnout: The three highest and three lowest councils (%)**

East Dunbartonshire	91.0	Glasgow	75.0
Stirling	90.1	Dundee	78.8
East Renfrewshire	90.4	Aberdeen	81.7

Table 2.4 **The four highest Yes votes (local authorities)**

	Yes (votes)	**Yes (%)**
Dundee	53,620	57.3
West Dunbartonshire	33,720	54.0
Glasgow	194,779	53.4
North Lanarkshire	115,783	51.1

Table 2.5 **The four highest No votes (local authorities)**

	No (votes)	**No (%)**
Orkney	10,004	67.2
Borders	55,553	66.5
Dumfries & Galloway	70,039	65.6
Shetland	9,951	63.6

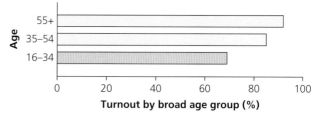

Figure 2.4 **Turnout by broad age group**

Table 2.6 **Gender, age and social class (%)**

	Men	**Women**	**60+**	**Under 60**	**ABC1**	**C2DE**
Yes	49	43	31	50.5	42	49
No	51	57	69	49.5	58	51

Source: Based on Lord Ashcroft poll and YouGov polls

Voting pattern

The initial two voting pattern polls taken by Lord Ashcroft and YouGov immediately after the referendum suggested that there was a clear split between older and young voters, male and female voters, and that low earners backed independence (see Table 2.6).

However, a new survey report published in September 2015 suggests that this was not the full picture. The report, based on a survey of 5,000 Scots and conducted a few days after the election, questioned some of the above assumptions. The survey suggests that the 'No' vote can be explained by an alliance of Scotland's younger voters, its average earners, Protestants and women.

Voters earning more than £30,000 were evenly split, while those earning less than £20,000 were 53 per cent for independence. The surprising figure was that those earning between £20,000 and £30,000 were only 44 per cent for independence. While it was true that the elderly favoured Scotland remaining part of the UK, the youngest voters, aged between 16 and 24, also delivered a 'No' to independence majority. Those aged 25 to 29 were the age group most likely to vote 'Yes', with 62 per cent for independence.

The survey also confirmed that those born in other parts of the UK but living in Scotland were overwhelmingly against independence with a resounding 70 per cent voting 'No'. Educational background had no significant impact. However, religious affiliation had a strong impact: 60 per cent of Protestants voted 'No', while 58 per cent of Catholics voted 'Yes'. The extreme Protestant organisation, the Orange Order, had campaigned for a 'No' vote and this partly explains the religious divergence.

Table 2.8 **Voting patterns by annual income (%)**

	Yes	No
£0–£19,999	53.2	46.8
£20,000–£29,999	45.5	54.5
£30,000–£39,999	49.8	50.2
Over £45,000	49.5	50.5

Source: Scottish Referendum Survey 2015

Role of the media

The media played an important part in the propaganda war between the two camps during this time. The 'Yes' camp was very effective in the use of social media including Twitter and had its own online magazine – *Bella Caledonia*.

New social media can be an avenue of misinformation, vile abuse and malicious propaganda. Cybernats – nationalist supporters – were accused of making abusive remarks towards prominent unionists such as J.K. Rowling, which damaged the nationalist cause. While the media gave massive coverage to attacks on Rowling and the entrepreneur Michelle Mone, cyber attacks on pro-independence females such as Elaine C. Smith failed to achieve much coverage in the media.

Newspapers

Newspaper coverage was mostly hostile to independence. The *Sunday Herald* became the only Scottish newspaper to openly support it. On 3 May 2014, in a striking front page designed by the Scottish writer and artist Alasdair Gray, the newspaper declared its support. The massive imbalance in support between the 'Yes' and 'No' campaigns was reflected in the referendum

Table 2.7 **Voting patterns by religious affiliation (%)**

	Yes	No
Protestant	39.9	60.1
Catholic	57.7	42.3
Church of England	19.4	80.6
Other	52.5	47.5
None	52.1	47.9

Source: Scottish Referendum Survey 2015

coverage in the press with negative stories dominating overall by about three to one. One absurd story published in the *Mirror* claimed that Edinburgh's giant pandas might have to be sent back to China if independence was achieved. The *Daily Express* front page headline of 8 June 2014 was: 'UK split to set back cure for cancer'. And again on 3 September: 'Yes vote risks EU veto and Wonga style interest rates'. Genuine Scottish newspapers such as the *Daily Record* were also guilty of scare-mongering stories: its headline on 12 September was that independence 'could trigger a new Great (world) Depression'.

Television

YouGov research highlighted the importance of television coverage of the referendum with a significant majority (71 per cent) stating that television and radio was their main source of information (see Figure 2.5). Central to the impact of television was the two television debates between the leaders of the campaigns and the BBC Big Debate which gave an opportunity for the 16–17 age group to express their opinions.

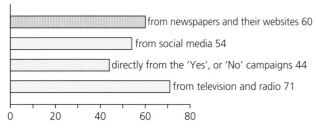

Figure 2.5 **Source of main information for Scottish voters**
Source: YouGov research for News UK

Key debates of 2014

5 August Victory for Alistair Darling over Alex Salmond. The former stated that Scotland would not have a currency union with the rest of the UK after independence and asked what would be the SNP's plan B when this happened. Salmond's answers were unconvincing and this was reflected in the ICM snap poll giving it to Darling by 56 per cent to 44 per cent.

25 August Victory this time for Alex Salmond. The SNP leader concentrated on issues such as the privatisation of the NHS, Trident and welfare cuts. This forced Darling to defend the UK Coalition Government policies with Salmond gleefully announcing that 'you're in bed with the Tories'. This view was reflected in the ICM/ *Guardian* opinion poll which gave victory to Salmond by 71 per cent to 29 per cent. This jibe would haunt Scottish Labour during the 2015 General Election campaign.

11 September The conventional view that 16- and 17-year-olds were not mature enough to engage in political debate was turned on its head after the BBC Big Debate which involved 7,500 16- and 17-year-olds listening to and questioning 'Yes' and 'No' politicians.

Show your understanding

1 Why was the Scottish Referendum described as a triumph for democracy?
2 Which groups in society were mostly likely to favour 'No', and which groups 'Yes', in the Scottish referendum?
3 Outline the influence of the media during the campaign.

Implications of the 2014 Scottish independence referendum

One of the most significant outcomes of the referendum was that the people of Scotland have become better engaged with politics. As Alex Salmond stated after the result was declared: 'Scotland now has the most politically engaged population in western Europe and one of the most engaged in any country, anywhere in the democratic world.' This is likely to have great implications for Scottish politics in the future.

In spite of the result, the referendum guaranteed major changes to the UK's constitutional structure with immediate calls for an English Parliament from some sections of society and a general consensus on the need for more regional powers to be granted across the UK. Lord Smith of Kelvin assumed responsibility for overseeing a new Scottish Devolution Commission to implement the cross-party decision to give more powers to Scotland.

The referendum result also affects people living in other parts of the union. The day after the result was declared David Cameron announced that he would use the outcome to implement longstanding Conservative plans to reform Commons rules to stop English MPs being overruled on English-only matters by the votes of Scottish MPs, settling the West Lothian question (see box below). All three main UK parties are broadly agreed on further powers for Scotland, but the 'English votes for English laws' plan is likely to prove highly controversial because of the danger of parliament having two classes of MPs.

The West Lothian question

The West Lothian question was asked by Tam Dalyell in 1977. It asks why Scottish MPs have the same right to vote at Westminster as any English MP now that large areas of policy are devolved to national parliaments and assemblies in areas such as health, housing, schools and policing.

Timescale September 2014–October 2015

18 September 2014 Scots reject independence. However, two days before the vote all three UK political leaders had promised further significant powers would be devolved. The *Daily Record*'s front page of 16 September called this 'The Vow' (see Figure 2.6). These new powers, it was claimed, would grant Scotland 'devo to the max' with only defence and economy management being left to Westminster.

19 September 2014 The Prime Minister set up a commission, under Lord Smith, to consider the implications of 'The Vow'. David Cameron also stated that the present situation whereby Scottish MPs in Westminster can vote on matters affecting English voters such as health (the West Lothian question) would be resolved.

27 November 2014 The Smith Commission announced its findings. Below are some of the main points:

- Increase financial accountability with the Scottish Parliament to have complete powers over income tax (the most unpopular of all taxes). It would also be allocated some share of VAT revenue.

- Increase the ability of the Scottish Parliament to tackle fuel poverty and promote energy efficiency.
- Control over a range of benefits including disability living allowance and the housing element of universal credit, including the bedroom tax.
- Control over airport passenger duty.
- The block grant to continue but to be reduced to take into consideration the income raised directly by the Scottish Government. The new funding formula should not be detrimental to Scotland. This new fiscal agreement to be in place before the new powers are transferred.

22 January 2015 The UK Government published draft powers to be granted to the Scottish Parliament which fall short of the Smith recommendations.

February 2015 William Hague, Conservative leader of the House of Commons, announced that English MPs should have a veto on legislation not applying to Scotland. This is referred to as EVEL – English votes for English laws (see below).

May 2015 The Conservatives won the election and formed a majority government. The SNP won 56 of the 59 Scottish seats.

October 2015 The Government's bill to introduce EVEL was passed by the House of Commons by 312 votes to 270. All MPs vote on the initial proposals. However, if the Speaker announces that it is an English-only issue, Scottish MPs will not be allowed to vote at the next stage of the bill.

Figure 2.6 The *Daily Record*, 16 Sep 2014. This vow is credited with persuading some voters who favoured devo-max to reject independence. Opinion polls in 2013-14 indicated that a majority of Scots wanted devo-max. According to Lord Ashcroft's post-referendum poll more than 20 per cent made their decision on this promise.

The implications of EVEL (English votes for English laws)

Critics argue that the decision to give English MPs a veto threatens the unity of the United Kingdom parliamentary system. It will create the situation as described in George Orwell's *Animal Farm* that 'all MPs are equal but some are more equal than others'. Scottish MPs will become second-class parliamentarians and the UK Parliament will become the English Parliament. Critics also point out that it is only in rare cases that Scottish votes have affected legislation that does not apply to Scotland. Between 2001 and 2015 Scottish MPs influenced only 25 of 3773 votes and most of these affected the entire United Kingdom. There is a strong argument that Scottish MPs should not vote on issues such as fox hunting in England. However, with Scotland having greater control over its finances, Conservative MPs wish to exclude Scottish MPS from voting on taxes and budgets. While these bills might at first glance apply to England, they will impact on Scotland's financial situation and should not be classed as English-only bills.

The first use of EVEL occurred in January 2016 when John Bercow, the Commons speaker, certified that large sections of the UK Government's Housing and Planning Bill related exclusively to England and would be considered by the new English Grand Committee. The Conservatives, however, seemed quite happy to use English Conservative MPs to vote down all the amendments to the Scotland Act supported by almost all Scottish MPs.

The Scotland Act 2016

In November 2015 the Scotland Act finally cleared the House of Commons. Only six hours was devoted to debating more than 800 amendments. The Conservative Scottish Secretary of State for Scotland, David Mundell, stated that the 'Vow' had now been delivered.

He rejected the SNP demand for full fiscal autonomy and for greater powers to be given to the Scottish Parliament. The only important amendment added to the original bill was the Conservative Government adding control of abortion laws to the new powers of the Scottish Parliament. However, all of the SNP amendments for greater powers were rejected including tax credits, graduate works visa scheme, industrial relations and workers' rights.

The bill went forward to the unelected House of Lords (it was boycotted by the SNP). After approval by the Lords, it was then discussed and approved by the Scottish Parliament (which can make no amendments to it). In March 2016 the royal assent was granted and the Act became law.

What powers are in the Scotland Act?

- The UK Government claims that this Act will make Holyrood the most devolved parliament in the world by granting it total control over income tax and aspects of VAT revenues and welfare.
- From 2017 the Scottish Parliament will have the power to set rates and bands of income tax, keep half of all its VAT receipts and be able to increase welfare payments and create new payments. New welfare powers are claimed to be worth about £2.5 billion. However, Universal Credit will remain a reserved benefit. Mr Mundell denied that this would give the UK Government a veto over these new welfare powers.
- The Scottish Parliament will be recognised as a permanent part of the constitution, with a referendum required to dissolve it.
- Ministers at Holyrood will have control over Scotland's abortion laws.
- Full devolution of Crown Estate with the exception of Fort Kinnaird in Edinburgh.
- The Act confirmed the greater borrowing powers for infrastructure spending arising from the Calman Report.

Criticism of the Scotland Act 2015

Critics argue that the allocation of control over only income tax is a poisoned chalice for the SNP. The Scottish Government will not be allocated fiscal control over less unpopular taxes such as corporation tax, excise duties, inheritance tax, fuel duties and all VAT revenues. The impact of the massive cuts to public expenditure, including welfare payments, will place severe pressures on the finances of the Scottish Parliament. Scotland has proportionately fewer high-earning people than England, and the Scottish population is falling relative to that of England. However, it does not have the power to increase immigration (migrants also contribute more in tax than they receive in benefits) which would help to counter the financial burden of an ageing population.

In short, with the further austerity cuts being imposed by the Conservative Government between 2015 and 2020, Scotland will have less income and will have to raise taxes in order to stay where it is. The massive reduction to welfare payments by the UK Government creates a dilemma and a paradox for the Scottish Government: it will have the powers to increase or create new benefits but not the ability to raise funds from, say, an increase in fuel tax, thus highlighting the flaws in the Scotland Bill. In contrast, it is now illegal for the UK Government to raise income tax in England and Wales. This is no accident as it removes the only escape route for the Scottish Government – an increase in income tax revenue across all of the UK. So, does the Scottish Government raise the unpopular income tax to safeguard welfare benefits and maintain public services, thus placing the Scottish taxpayers in an unfair financial position compared to English taxpayers; or does it do nothing and be blamed for cuts in all of the above services? This explains why the new fiscal arrangement agreed by the two governments is so crucial.

The new fiscal framework (Barnett Formula)

At present Scotland receives an increase in its block grant in proportion to the increase in spending on UK departments. With the new income tax and VAT revenues to be devolved, adjustments will have to be made to the annual £30 billion block grant to reflect this new income source. The Smith Commission stated that the new fiscal arrangements should not be financially detrimental to either Scotland or the rest of the UK. The UK Government's view is that their 'level funding' proposed framework is advantageous to Scotland in its first year – Scotland would receive more than it would have done under the Barnett Formula. And this framework will be adjusted depending on the population growths in the respective countries. However, population growth is greater in England and this formula would over a period of time be detrimental to Scotland. John Swinney, the then Scottish Financial Secretary, stated that, over a 10-year period, Scotland would lose £3 billion.

John Swinney prefers a 'per capita indexation' framework which would protect Scotland's finances from a slower population growth than England. This formula was endorsed by the Scottish MPs on the SNP-chaired Commons Scottish Affairs Committee. John Swinney is also concerned about the amount a Scottish Government could borrow to protect public services if a recession were to occur (income tax revenue slumps during a recession). While the Smith Commission stated that Holyrood 'should have additional borrowing powers to ensure budgetary stability and provide safeguards to smooth Scottish public spending in the event of economic shocks' it did not specify a new borrowing limit. The Scotland Bill does not provide clarity on this issue.

The compromise agreement

Finally, a compromise agreement was reached in late February 2016, which in many ways postponed a final agreement for a further five years. The key points were:

- The treasury mechanism is to be used but tweaked to ensure that Scotland would not lose out (so, in reality, the John Swinney mechanism).
- The transitional fund to cover the setting up of a new tax and welfare system is to be increased from £50 million to £200 million.
- After five years of this interim agreement a final agreement will be mutually agreed between the two governments.

Show your understanding

1 What was the impact of the referendum on the demand for further powers and the status of Scottish MPs in the House of Commons?
2 Outline the powers granted to the Scottish Parliament by the Scotland Act 2015 and criticisms made of these powers.
3 Why was it difficult to agree to a new block grant formula and what was the outcome?

12-mark question

Analyse the impact of the Scotland Act 2015 on the powers of the Scottish Parliament.

Electoral systems

The purpose of elections

In a democracy, citizens can participate freely through voting to elect their representatives.

Elections provide legitimacy to the winning party and to the political system as a whole. By voting, we give consent even if our candidates lose. We can influence the policies of the different parties, and the government of the day will face accountability at the next election.

The failure of the first past the post (FPTP) electoral system to produce a clear winner in the May 2010 General Election once again opened the debate over its relevance in the UK in the twenty-first century. As part of the agreement between the Conservatives and Liberal Democrats, a referendum was held on whether the alternative vote (AV) system should be adopted (see pages 35–36). Under the agreement, the Conservatives were free to campaign against change. Many critics would have preferred the choice to be between FPTP and a proportional representation (PR) system, rather than AV (a modified version of FPTP). The decision to hold the referendum on the same day as the May 2011 Holyrood elections was criticised in Scotland.

All the opinion polls prior to the 2015 General Election predicted another 'hung parliament'. However, to everyone's surprise, the Conservatives achieved an overall majority, and formed a single party government – FPTP had delivered majority government again!

Figure 3.1 **Voters taking part in the 2015 General Election**

In the past, the UK had only one electoral system – FPTP – and this was used to elect MPs to the House of Commons, councillors to local councils across the UK and representatives to the European Parliament.

However, this is no longer the case. As Table 3.1 indicates, a variety of PR systems now operate within the UK for various elections. In Scotland we elect local councillors using the single transferable vote (STV), a form of PR; at present we elect our representatives to the European Parliament using the regional list, also a form of PR; we elect Members of the Scottish Parliament (MSPs) using the additional member system (AMS), a mixture of FPTP and PR; and finally we elect our Members of Parliament (MPs) to the House of Commons using FPTP. So it is no surprise that there is great debate about what system is best for the UK.

Table 3.1 **Electoral systems in use in the UK in 2016**

System	Election of	Constituency type (single- or multi-member)
First past the post (FPTP)	House of Commons Local government Councils in England and Wales (not Scotland)	Single
Additional member system (AMS)	Scottish Parliament Welsh Assembly London Assembly	Single and multi
Regional list	European Parliament (not Northern Ireland)	Multi
Single transferable vote (STV)	Scottish local government councils, Northern Ireland Assembly, European Parliament (Northern Ireland only)	Multi

What should an election deliver?

- Should it be a FPTP system that usually helps to deliver a clear winner and strong government, and maintains an effective link between MPs and geographical constituencies?
- Or should it be a PR system that helps to ensure greater proportionality and fairness between votes cast and seats achieved?

First past the post

FPTP is a simple plurality system and is the most important electoral system in the UK because it is used for Westminster general elections. The UK is divided into 650 single-member constituencies, also known as 'seats', and each one elects an MP. The candidate with the most votes becomes the MP.

Table 3.2 illustrates why FPTP is referred to as the 'winner-takes-all' system. In 2015, the Labour candidate won the City of Chester seat with a

majority of only 65. Similarly, in the 1992 General Election, 74 per cent of voters in the constituency of Inverness, Nairn and Lochaber did not vote for the winning candidate.

Table 3.2 **City of Chester 2015**

	Votes	Share (%)
Labour	22,118	43.2
Conservative	22,025	43.1
UKIP	4,148	8.1
Liberal Democrats	2,870	5.6

There are no prizes for coming second in this system. For example, in the 2015 General Election UKIP came second in 120 constituencies and received more than 3.8 million votes. Their reward for such a spectacular performance was one seat in the House of Commons!

Differences in the size of constituencies can reflect geographic factors. The Isle of Wight has the most electors and the Western Isles the fewest. Historically, Scotland has been over-represented, and the number of Scottish constituencies was reduced from 72 to 59 in 2005.

Figure 3.2 **The declaration in Thanet South in 2015:** UKIP leader Nigel Farage failed to win the seat.

The bill to hold the May 2011 referendum on electoral reform, which was part of the coalition deal between the Conservatives and Liberal Democrats, also included plans to redraw constituency boundaries to create as far as possible numerically equal constituencies of around 75,000 voters. (The two main exceptions are the Scottish seats of Orkney and Shetland, and the Western Isles.) This proposal would have reduced the number of constituencies from 650 to 600 and would have favoured the Conservative Party. Independent experts have calculated that with 50 fewer MPs, Labour would lose around 27 seats, the Conservatives around 12, the Liberal Democrats around 5 and other parties the remaining 6.

However, the Liberal Democrats withdrew their support for boundary reform. Backbench Tory MPs were against the Coalition bill to reform the House of Lords, and so David Cameron was forced to drop the bill to avoid a Conservative rebellion. It is expected that boundary reform will be reintroduced in the 2015–20 Parliament.

Features of FPTP

Maintains a two-party system

FPTP ensures that the proportion of seats won by Conservative and Labour is far greater than the proportion of votes they receive. In the 2015 General Election the combined Conservative/ Labour vote was 69.0 per cent yet they received 85.0 per cent of the seats (see Table 3.3). Some political commentators argue that FPTP acts as a life-support machine for the two-party system and distorts the will of the electorate.

The figures in bold denote the share of the vote of the party that won the most seats in the House of Commons. In 1951 and 1974 the party with the most votes did not win the most seats.

Table 3.3 **The British two-party system, selected years**

| | Share of the vote (%) | | | Share of the seats (%) | | | Liberal / Liberal Democrats | | Overall majority |
	Con	Lab	Con + Lab	Con	Lab	Con + Lab	Votes (%)	Seats (%)	
1951	48.0	**48.8**	96.8	51.4	47.2	98.6	2.5	1.0	17
1974*	**37.9**	37.1	75.0	46.6	47.4	94.0	19.3	2.2	–
1974*	35.8	**39.2**	75.0	43.5	50.2	93.7	18.3	2.0	3
1983	**42.4**	27.6	70.0	61.0	32.2	93.2	25.4	3.6	144
1992	**41.9**	34.4	76.3	51.6	41.6	93.2	17.9	3.1	21
1997	30.7	**43.2**	73.9	25.0	63.6	88.6	16.8	7.0	179
2001	31.7	**40.7**	72.4	25.1	62.6	87.7	18.8	7.9	167
2010	**36.1**	29.0	65.1	47.2	38.7	85.9	23.0	8.9	–
2015	**36.8**	30.4	67.2	50.1	35.0	85.0	7.9	1.2	12

*Two elections were held in 1974.

Comfortable government

FPTP usually exaggerates the performance of the most popular party and provides it with a comfortable majority in parliament.

The Conservatives under Margaret Thatcher enjoyed landslide victories in 1983 and 1987, as did Labour under Tony Blair in 1997 and 2001.

Unfair to smaller parties

FPTP discriminates against third parties and smaller parties whose support is spread across the UK but is not concentrated in particular regions. The Liberal Democrats have consistently suffered: there are no rewards for coming second in, for example, 300 constituencies. In the 2010 General Election, the Liberal Democrats won 23 per cent of the vote but received only 57 seats; in contrast, Labour won 29 per cent of the vote and received 307 seats. In 2015, UKIP and the Green Party received a combined total of five million votes, yet only received one seat each.

Limited choice

Many constituencies are safe seats, in which one party has a massive majority over its rivals and is unlikely to lose. All of Glasgow's Westminster constituencies are now held by the SNP, and the Conservatives do very badly. Why should a Conservative supporter bother to vote when his or her vote will be of no consequence? Voters whose favoured party has little support might engage in tactical voting. Instead of voting for their party, electors cast their votes for the candidate best placed to prevent a party they dislike from winning the seat.

Favours parties whose votes are concentrated

The SNP were the clear beneficiaries of having all their votes concentrated in only 59 of the 650 UK constituencies. In Scotland the SNP with 50 per cent of the Scottish votes (1.4 million votes) gained 95 per cent of the seats. In contrast UKIP with more than 3.8 million votes (12.9 per cent of votes) gained only one seat. In Scotland, UKIP received only 1.6 per cent of the votes (47,000).

Traditionally the Liberal Democrats fared better in Scotland than in the rest of the UK. In 2010 the SNP vote was 491,386 compared to the Liberal Democrats' 465,471 – yet the Liberal Democrats won eleven seats and the SNP only six. In Scotland in 2015 the Conservatives won 15 per cent of the vote but only one of the 59 seats.

Table 3.4 **Average number of votes needed to win a constituency at the 2015 General Election**

	Number of votes	
Party	UK	Scotland
Conservative	34,244	434,097
Labour	40,290	707,147
Liberal Democrats	301,986	219,675
SNP	–	25,972

Clearly, in Scotland FPTP now favours the SNP rather than Labour. In the 2010 Scottish results, it only took about 25,000 votes to elect a Labour MP in Scotland; now it is 707,147.

The 2010 General Election

The Conservatives prevented Labour from winning four general elections in a row but it was to be no landslide victory for the Conservatives and no breakthrough by the Liberal Democrats.

The most significant feature of the 2010 General Election was the failure of FPTP to deliver on its main promise – a single-party government. The last time a hung parliament had occurred was in February 1974.

A total of 326 seats is needed for a party to form a majority government. The Conservative Party achieved only 307 seats and as such formed a

Arguments for FPTP

1 It exaggerates the performance of the most popular party, producing a winner's dividend and even a landslide victory. In 1997, Labour won 43 per cent of the vote and gained 419 seats in the House of Commons, giving them a massive majority.

2 Strong single-party government allows the prime minister and Cabinet to pursue the policies they stated clearly in their election manifesto without having to compromise with smaller parties in the coalitions associated with PR. The 2015 Conservative manifesto promised a referendum and this took place in 2016.

3 FPTP prevents extremist parties from obtaining representation. The British National Party (BNP) achieved over half a million votes in the 2010 General Election but gained no seats. Under a PR system, the BNP won two seats in the 2009 European elections.

4 When an MP retires or dies, a by-election is held to elect a new MP. This enables the public to show their disapproval of a government or a party that has become unpopular. In December 2015 the first by-election of the new UK Parliament was held. Labour had elected a new leader, Jeremy Corbyn, who had received a very negative press. Labour easily retained the seat and this was regarded as a vote of confidence in the new leader.

5 It is easy to understand and implement. Electors only vote once and the results are announced very quickly. In contrast, there were 140,000 spoilt ballot papers in the 2007 Scottish Parliament elections.

Arguments against FPTP

1 The two-party system is past its sell-by date because it no longer reflects voting patterns. In the 1950s, more than 90 per cent of the electorate voted for either of the two major parties; in the 2015 General Election, less than 70 per cent of the electorate voted for either the Conservatives or Labour. It is unfair to third and minority parties: in 2015 UKIP received over 3.8 million votes but only received one seat.

2 FPTP does not always produce a victory for the party with the most votes or deliver a fair or decisive result. In the February 1974 election, the Conservatives gained more votes than Labour yet had fewer seats (see Table 3.3). In the 2015 election, the Conservatives formed a government with less than 40 per cent of the votes cast. Again in 2010, FPTP failed to deliver a decisive outcome.

3 Strong government does not always create a good or fair government. When FPTP was used in the elections in Northern Ireland, the leader of the Ulster Unionists made the infamous statement 'a Protestant government for a Protestant people'. This abuse of power denied Northern Irish Catholics their civil and political rights. Today in Northern Ireland, under a PR system (STV), there is a power-sharing government between the Democratic Unionist Party and Sinn Fein.

4 The winning MP may not have a majority of the votes cast; indeed, they may receive less than 30 per cent of the vote. In 1992, the Liberal Democrat candidate in Inverness East, Nairn and Lochaber won with 26 per cent of the vote.

5 FPTP in the 2015 General Election exaggerated differences and created division and tension between the nations of the UK. The UK parties in Scotland received just under 50 per cent of the votes but received only five per cent of the seats.

coalition government with David Cameron as prime minister and Nick Clegg (the Liberal Democrat leader) as deputy prime minister. The Conservatives also offered to hold a referendum on the introduction of the AV system to replace FPTP.

The key statistics of the 2010 General Election illustrate the contrasting fortunes of the major parties:

- The Conservatives gained 87 seats from Labour and 12 from the Liberal Democrats.
- Labour's 29 per cent share of the UK vote was only slightly better than the party's post-war low in 1983.
- The drift away from the 'old two-party system' continued: only two in three of all votes cast were for the two major parties.

The 2015 General Election

Despite all the predictions of a 'hung parliament', David Cameron obtained an overall majority to enable the Conservatives to govern alone – they increased their seats by 24 (see Table 3.5). Gains in the Conservative vote were largely concentrated in the Liberal Democrat seats, and in contrast Labour losses were concentrated in Scotland. The new Government's working majority was only 12 and it was predicted that this might create future problems for David Cameron. The election witnessed the emergence of multi-party politics with seven leaders taking part in televised debates. The 2015–20 Parliament holds a record number of female and BME (black or minority ethnic) MPs. Female MPs make up

Table 3.5 **Result of the 2015 General Election: UK turnout 66.1%**

Party	Seats	Gain	Loss	Net	Votes	Vote(%)	+/–
Conservative	331	35	11	+24	11,334,576	36.9	+0.8
Labour	232	22	48	−26	9,347,304	30.4	+1.5
SNP	56	50	0	+50	1,454,436	4.7	+3.1
Liberal Democrat	8	0	49	-49	2,415,862	7.9	−15.2
UKIP	1	1	0	+1	3,881,099	12.6	+9.5
Green	1	0	0	0	1,157,613	3.8	+2.8

Table 3.6 **Result of the 2015 General Election: Scotland turnout 71.1%**

Party	Seats	Gain	Loss	Votes	Vote (%)	+/–
SNP	56	50	0	1,454,436	50.0	+30.0
Labour	1	0	40	707,147	24.3	−17.7
Conservative	1	0	0	434,097	14.9	−1.8
Liberal Democrat	1	0	10	219,675	7.5	−11.3
UKIP	0	0	0	47,078	1.6	+0.9
Green	0	0	0	39,205	1.3	+0.7

28.2 per cent, up from 22.8 per cent, and BME MPs 6.3 per cent, up from 4.2 per cent. Mhairi Black, SNP, became the youngest MP at the age of 20 ever to sit in the UK Parliament.

It was a strange election which highlighted the inconsistencies and shortcomings of FPTP. Labour increased its percentage of votes but suffered a loss in seats. UKIP gained more than 3.8 million votes but was rewarded with only one seat. In Scotland the Unionist parties – Labour, the Conservatives and Liberal Democrats – gained a combined vote of just under 50 per cent of the votes, yet only received 5 per cent of the seats. The Green Party won more than one million votes and retained their one seat. It is no wonder the Electoral Reform Society stated that 'this was the most disproportionate result in British election history'. The make-up of Parliament clearly demonstrates the massive divide in voting behaviour between Scotland and England.

For many, FPTP had once again delivered unrepresentative government. The Tories maintained power with only 37 per cent of the vote – the same figure with which Labour had lost power in 1979. Moreover only 24 per cent of those on the electoral roll had voted Conservative. In England and Wales, one-third of the electorate did not vote for either the Conservatives or Labour, yet between them they won 98 per cent of the seats. The Scottish people once again overwhelmingly rejected Conservative rule only to be controlled by a Conservative Government determined to slash the Scottish budget.

At first glance the results seemed to be a return to the two-party system; the share of the vote won by the Conservatives and Labour increased from 66.7 per cent to 69 per cent and the Conservatives were rewarded with an overall majority. For supporters of FPTP the system had delivered stable government provided by the most popular party, offering clear accountability.

Yet, nearly one in every four voters voted for parties outwith the traditional big three, more than twice the highest total of 11 per cent recorded in 2010. The electorate had clearly embraced multi-party policies, but FPTP rejected their wishes. The distortion between votes cast and seats secured was best illustrated in the results in England and Wales. Here the traditional big three parties won 98 per cent of the available seats.

The 2015 General Election witnessed the collapse of support for the Liberal Democrats – in terms of votes UKIP became the third largest party in the UK. The Liberal Democrats lost 49 seats and five million voters, and were reduced to a party of eight MPs. Their decision to become junior members of the 2010–15 Coalition Government condemned the party to near electoral oblivion. Its leader and former Deputy Prime Minister Nick Clegg resigned after the election.

UKIP might have overtaken the Liberal Democrats in terms of votes, but this was of little comfort as the party received only one seat. It only managed to win the Clacton seat that the Conservative defector, Douglas Carswell, had won in 2014 in a by-election. UKIP leader Nigel Farage had failed to win in Thanet South – he finished second with 32 per cent of the vote. UKIP also failed to retain the Kent seat of Rochester and Strood, which it had won at a by-election during the autumn of 2014. UKIP came second in 112 constituencies and won almost 13 per cent of the votes. UKIP's vote was too evenly spread across the country to come first in any constituency. It also did badly in London and Scotland – the vast majority of UKIP's worst results were in Scotland.

Ed Miliband resigned as the Labour leader after a 'very disappointing night'. Shadow Chancellor Ed Balls and the Scottish Labour leader, Jim

Murphy, both lost their seats. Labour slightly increased their UK votes but still lost an overall 26 seats (blamed on the 'tartan tsunami'!). The Conservative strategy, supported by the Tory press such as the *Daily Mail*, to portray Ed Miliband as being in the pocket of the SNP persuaded some voters to switch to the Conservatives. Opinion polls had suggested that no party would have an overall majority and that the SNP would hold the balance of power.

Scotland: The referendum dividend

The results in Scotland witnessed a tartan tsunami that swept away Labour's dominance and all the traditional theories of voting behaviour. The SNP's number of seats rose from 6 to a staggering 56; in contrast Labour dropped from 40 to 1. In some former Labour safe seats the electoral swing to the SNP was more than 35 per cent. The SNP polled more than 50 per cent of the votes in 33 seats. The Liberal Democrats lost 10 of their 11 seats to the SNP. The Conservatives witnessed a drop in their electoral support but managed to retain their one seat held by David Mundell, who became the Secretary of State for Scotland.

Alternative vote

This was the electoral system proposed by the Liberal Democrats to replace FPTP in 2010. This seemed a strange choice for the Liberal Democrats because AV is, in effect, only a modified form of FPTP. Research by the Electoral Reform Society indicates that the Liberal Democrats would have won an additional 22 seats if AV had been used in the 2010 General Election, and 105 more under STV. Table 3.7 indicates what the results would have been under different voting systems in 2015.

Table 3.7 **The number of seats won by each party in the 2015 General Election under different voting systems**

Party	First past the post	Alternative vote	Single transferable vote
Conservative	331	337	276
Labour	232	227	236
Liberal Democrats	8	9	26
UKIP	1	1	54

AV is used to elect Australia's lower house, the House of Representatives, and in the UK it is used to elect the leader of the Labour Party and Liberal Democrats. In AV the winning candidate has to achieve an overall majority of the votes cast. Voters write '1' beside the name of their first-choice candidate, '2' next to their second choice and so on. Voters may decide to vote only for their first choice. If no candidate has secured an absolute majority of first preferences, the lowest-placed candidate drops out and the second preferences of his or her votes are transferred to the remaining candidates. If this does not produce a candidate with more than 50 per cent of the votes, the procedure will be repeated until it does.

Arguments for AV
- It would not require any boundary changes and the constituencies would still return one MP.
- All MPs would have gained the majority of the votes and they would have broader support.

Arguments aganist AV
- The candidate who secures the most first-preference votes may not be elected when second or third preferences have been distributed.
- It retains all the weaknesses of FPTP and is still unfair to third and minority parties.

Alternative Vote referendum 2011

The country voted 'No' to changing the electoral system and chose to continue to support a FPTP system that they understood. The Liberal Democrats and the 'Yes' campaign failed to match the impact of the 'No' campaign supported by the Conservative Party and some Labour politicians, such as John Reid. No region had a majority of 'Yes' votes; only in Northern Ireland did the 'Yes' vote muster a respectable figure (see Table 3.8). Of the 440 UK voting areas only ten, including Glasgow Kelvin and Edinburgh Central, voted 'Yes'.

The turnout at the referendum was also low, reflecting the 'Yes' campaign's failure to capture the interest of the public. It was clear that much of the public did not understand the Alternative Vote System. Northern Ireland had the highest turnout at 56 per cent, followed by Scotland at 51 per cent. London had the lowest turnout at only 35 per cent.

The Liberal Democrats were also unhappy at the tactics of the 'No' campaign and the Conservative leaders. At the beginning of the campaign David Cameron indicated he would not fight Mr Clegg head to head over the referendum. However, early 2011 opinion polls gave the 'Yes' vote a clear lead and to placate the right-wingers in his party Mr Cameron threw his weight behind the 'No' campaign.

The Prime Minister did not disown the blatant lies proclaimed by the 'No' campaign – that new ballot boxes would be needed, that the cost of AV would be astronomical and that a party that came last, such as the British National Party (BNP), could end up having the winning candidate. However, Labour did not blame the Conservatives for the failed referendum. Labour's Ben Bradshaw tweeted: 'Done countless AV meetings in recent months. Two words sum up the reason for the scale of defeats: Nick Clegg. Toxic. Specially with Labour voters.'

Table 3.8 AV referendum results by UK nation states, May 2011

Nation	Yes (%)	No (%)	Turnout (%)
England	32.1	67.9	42.2
Scotland	36.3	63.6	50.7
Northern Ireland	43.7	56.3	55.8
Wales	34.5	65.4	41.7

Scottish referendum

In September 2014 a referendum was held in Scotland on the issue of Scotland leaving the UK and becoming an independent country (see pages 16–24 for an in-depth coverage).

Table 3.9 Should Scotland be an independent country?

	Votes	%
Yes	1,617,989	44.7
No	2,001,926	55.3

Show your understanding

1 Describe the different electoral systems used in the UK.
2 Why is the UK electoral system referred to as first past the post?
3 Refer to Table 3.3. Examine the statements below and indicate to what extent you agree, or disagree, with each:
   a) There has been a significant decline in support for the two major parties.
   b) All elections since 1951 have produced a clear winner.
   c) The Liberal Democrats have been unfairly treated by FPTP.
4 Outline the main features of FPTP and evaluate the arguments for and against PR.
5 Outline the advantages and disadvantages of AV.
6 Analyse the results of the 2011 AV referendum.

Proportional representation

Arguments for PR

1 PR is 'fair' because it produces a close correlation between share of the vote and share of seats. The Conservatives received over 22 per cent of the votes and 24 per cent of the seats in the 2016 Scottish Parliament elections.

2 PR gives minor parties more parliamentary representation and encourages voters to vote for them without feeling that their votes will be wasted. In the 2003 elections for the Scottish Parliament, AMS enabled the Scottish Socialist Party (SSP), the Green Party, the Scottish Senior Citizens Unity Party and the independents to be represented.

3 Coalition government increases the percentage of the electorate supporting the government parties. In the 2010 General Election, the coalition Conservative–Liberal Democrat Government won a combined 59 per cent of votes.

4 Coalitions encourage consensus, which is the result of compromise. In other words, more voters get some of what they want and less of what they do not want. The Liberal Democrats and Labour formed a coalition government in Scotland in 1999–2007, providing stable and effective government. The UK Coalition Government of 2010–15 was also regarded as stable and effective.

5 Some people argue that PR will reduce the number of 'wasted votes' and so encourage greater turnout.

Arguments against PR

1 PR can create a government in which a minority party can implement its policies. The Liberal Democrats finished fourth in the 2003 Scottish election, yet formed a government with Labour. When they formed a coalition with the Conservatives in May 2010, the Liberal Democrats dropped their manifesto pledges such as no increase in student fees.

2 PR can lead to an unstable and weak government. The minority SNP Government of 2007–11 found it difficult to implement some of its policies. For example, it failed to implement its policy of minimum pricing of alcohol in November 2010.

3 PR does not always create a more representative Scottish Parliament. In the 2007 Scottish elections, the number of MSPs outwith the four major parties decreased from 17 to 3.

4 Some people argue that AMS creates conflict between the constituency MSP and the seven list MSPs. There is clear rivalry between the two classes of MSPs.

5 The regional list system makes parties more powerful than voters. Being placed first or second on your party's list will mean you have a very good chance of being elected to the Scottish Parliament (assuming you represent one of the major parties). Margo MacDonald, a leading SNP figure, decided to stand as an independent on the Lothian regional list after she had been given a low place on the SNP's party list.

The additional member system

The AMS mixed electoral system has been used to elect the Scottish Parliament and Welsh Assembly since 1999, and also the London Assembly. In Scotland the voters cast two votes. The first vote is to elect the 73 winning candidates in the local constituency elections using FPTP.

Voters also have a second vote in a multi-member constituency, choosing between parties. Scotland is divided into eight regional lists, each electing seven regional list MSPs (see Figure 3.3). The d'Hondt formula is used to ensure that the number of seats for parties in the Scottish Parliament is roughly proportional to the number of votes they won. A party that has a clear lead in the constituency election will do less well in the regional list elections. In 2007 Labour won 37 constituency seats but only 9 regional list seats.

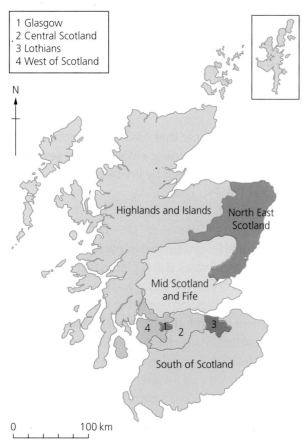

1 Glasgow
2 Central Scotland
3 Lothians
4 West of Scotland

N

Highlands and Islands
North East Scotland
Mid Scotland and Fife
4 1 2 3
South of Scotland

0   100 km

Figure 3.3 **The eight multi-member constituencies in Scotland**

The outcome is that a single party hardly ever wins a majority of seats. AMS ensured the creation of Labour and Liberal Democrat coalition governments after the 1999 and 2003 elections and a minority SNP Government after the 2007 election. In 2016 the SNP won 59 constituency seats but only 4 regional list seats. In contrast, Labour won only 3 constituency seats but won 21 regional list seats. The 2011 and 2016 Scottish Parliament results are highlighted on pages 39–42.

Impact of the Scottish Parliament voting system

AMS, incorporating a strong element of PR, was introduced to reduce the alleged deficiencies of FPTP. What have been the principal consequences for Scottish politics of its operation since 1999?

A fairer result

There is no doubt that AMS increases proportionality by reducing the gap between share of votes and share of seats. In sharp contrast, in 2010 the FPTP system awarded Labour almost 70 per cent of Scottish seats in the House of Commons with only 42 per cent of the Scottish votes and in 2015 the SNP won 95 per cent of the Scottish seats with only 50 per cent of the votes.

Coalition government or minority-party government

In 1999 and 2003, Labour formed a coalition government with the Liberal Democrats.

In the 2007 election, the SNP overtook Labour as the strongest party in the Scottish Parliament, but only by a single seat. The SNP could not find a coalition partner with enough seats to provide a parliamentary majority. The SNP formed a minority government and had to depend on other parties supporting their policies for the respective bills to be passed in Parliament.

Small parties encouraged and sometimes rewarded

In 2003, the Greens and the SSP won 13 out of 56 seats in the second ballot. The presence of Green and SSP MSPs in the Scottish Parliament would not have been achieved under FPTP.

This feature has been erratic in so far as the significant gains of both the Greens and the SSP in 2003 were almost eliminated in 2007, when they lost votes and seats as the SNP surged into first place. Thanks to AMS, the Greens hung on in 2011 with 2 list seats, and in 2016 won 6 seats.

Greater voter choice

There has been a large increase in the number of parties and individual candidates competing for seats in the second ballot. No fewer than 23 parties and independents contested the second ballot in both Glasgow and the Lothians in 2016.

The second ballot and an increase in the number of parties have given voters the opportunity to vote for more than one party. However, the 2007 and 2011 results emphasise that smaller parties are not guaranteed representation if the battle between the major parties intensifies, meaning that their share of the second-ballot regional vote falls below 5–6 per cent.

Parties rewarded for votes achieved

AMS has maintained the four-party character of Scottish politics by coming to the rescue of the Conservatives. The Conservatives won only one seat in the 2010 General Election; in contrast, they have 15 MSPs in the Scottish Parliament of 2011–16.

Can still deliver majority government

The UK-based parties assumed and were happy to accept that AMS would ensure no one party won an overall majority (this would prevent the SNP in forming a strong government). However, in 2011 the SNP swept to power with a clear parliamentary majority. In 2016 the SNP won 63 seats, narrowly missing the required 65 seats to achieve a majority government.

Gender representation in the Scottish Parliament

One of the most striking features of the first election to the Scottish Parliament in 1999 was that 48 of the 129 MSPs were women – 37 per cent of the total membership. This was double the proportion of women in the House of Commons and close to the 40 per cent achieved in Sweden. In both the 2011 and 2016 elections, 45 women MSPs were elected.

Electorate confusion

The May 2007 Scottish Parliament and local council elections created confusion among the electorate. A change to the ballot papers for the parliamentary elections and a switch from FPTP to STV for local council elections seemed to confuse some voters. In the 2003 elections there had been 45,700 rejected ballot papers; in the 2007 elections, a staggering 140,000 were rejected. This was not an issue in the subsequent 2011 and 2016 elections.

Scottish Parliament election, May 2011

Alex Salmond's landslide victory took everyone by surprise. In January 2010 early opinion polls gave Labour a clear 16 points lead. This was confirmed in the 2010 General Election when Scottish Labour easily dismissed the SNP challenge and, in fact, Scotland was the only part of the UK where Labour's vote increased.

When the Scottish Parliament elections came around in May 2011, the SNP gained 22 seats and achieved what was regarded as impossible under the proportional voting system – an overall majority of seats: 69 out of 129. In the north-east, the SNP won all 10 constituency seats, and still obtained another on the regional list. The results were all the more remarkable given that in the 1999 election the then-dominant Labour Party achieved only 56 seats.

A Labour aide, speaking after the results were announced, described the situation as 'ground zero', especially for several high-profile MSPs. Labour's decision not to use the regional list as a safety net for the party heavyweights left it without its most experienced and talented MSPs.

Scottish voters punished the Liberal Democrats for their coalition with the Conservatives in Westminster and the party was reduced from 16 MSPs to 5, with no mainland constituency MSPs. (Shetland and Orkney returned the two Liberal Democrat constituency MSPs, including the then-leader Tavish Scott.) Overall the party's vote slumped below half its 2007 level with Liberal Democrat disaffected voters switching to the SNP. It was also a disappointing result for the Conservatives and a slight disappointment for the Greens. Conservative support fell to its lowest level in Scotland and the party lost two of its MSPs. The number of Green MSPs did not increase after the election but they were able to retain their two MSPs.

Why did Labour suffer such a massive defeat?

1 The original strategy to ignore the SNP and instead campaign against the UK Coalition and the return to Thatcherism was a disaster. The tactics that worked in the 2010 General Election failed to impress the electorate this time around.

2 The SNP campaign confirmed Alex Salmond's popularity and leadership qualities. In a YouGov poll in April 2011, 52 per cent of those asked said Mr Salmond would make the best first minister. Only 27 per cent chose Mr Gray, the Labour leader, who was regarded as the invisible, dull politician.

3 The collapse of the Liberal Democrat vote benefited the SNP rather than Labour, dramatically changing the Scottish political map. The Liberal Democrats lost 11 of their 16 MSPs and retained only their constituency MSPs in Orkney and Shetland. Labour's constituency votes remained solid with only a 0.5 per cent reduction, yet they lost 22 of their constituency MSPs.

Table 3.10 **Summary of total MSPs by party from 1999 to 2011**

Party	1999	2003	2007	2011
SNP	35	27	47	69
Labour	56	50	46	37
Conservative	18	18	17	15
Liberal Democrats	17	17	16	5
Green	1	7	2	2
SSP	1	6	0	0
Others	1	4	1	1

Table 3.11 **Scottish Parliament election results May 2011**

Party	SNP	+/−	Lab	+/−	Cons	+/−	Liberal Democrat	+/−	Other	+/−
Total	69	+22	37	−9	15	−2	5	−11	3	−

Scottish Parliamentary Election 2016

As predicted the SNP won a third election in a row, with 63 seats, but just failed to win an overall majority. The d'Hont system, designed to prevent the winning party gaining an overall majority, had worked. However, what was not predicted was the Conservative party pushing Labour into third place.

The SNP increased its votes and seats in the constituency results. The SNP vote was up 1.1 per cent on 2011, winning 59 of Scotland's 73 first-past-the-post seats, an increase of six. It narrowly missed being higher – the SNP just failed to win Dumbarton and Edinburgh Southern. This would have given the SNP an overall majority. As it was, the d'Hont regional list system punished the SNP for gaining over a million constituency votes and 80 per cent of the constituency seats. Despite gaining almost 940,000 regional votes, the SNP received only 4 regional seats; in 6 of the 8 regions, the SNP got no list MSPs (in contrast, the Conservatives with 524,000 regional votes won 24 regional seats).

Table 3.12 Scottish Parliament election results May 2016

Party	SNP	+/−	Lab	+/−	Cons	+/−	Liberal Democrats	+/−	Green	+/−
Total	63	−6	24	−13	31	+16	5	−	6	+4

Table 3.13 Scottish Parliament election May 2016 constituency results

Party	Seats	+/−	Votes	%	+/− %
SNP	59	+6	1,059,877	46.5	+1.1
Labour	3	−12	514,261	22.6	−9.1
Conservative	7	+4	501,844	22.0	+8.1
Liberal Democrats	4	+2	178,238	7.8	−0.1
Greens	0	−	13,172	0.6	−

Table 3.14 Scottish Parliament election May 2016 regional list results

Party	Seats	+/−	Votes	%	+/− %
SNP	4	−12	953,587	41.7	−2.3
Labour	21	−1	435,919	19.1	−7.2
Conservative	24	+12	524,222	22.9	+10.5
Liberal Democrats	1	−2	115,284	5.2	−
Greens	6	+4	150,426	6.6	+2.3

Table 3.15 **Scottish Parliament election May 2016 parliamentary region results**

Region	SNP	Labour	Conservative	Liberal Democrats	Green
Highlands and Islands	7	2	3	2	1
North East Scotland	9	2	5	1	–
Mid Scotland and Fife	8	2	4	1	1
Central	9	4	3	–	–
Lothians	6	3	4	1	2
Glasgow	9	4	2	–	1
West of Scotland	8	4	4	–	1
South Scotland	7	3	6	–	–
Total	63	24	31	5	6

Under the leadership of Ruth Davidson (her name was placed on the ballot papers), the Conservatives played the unionist card and claimed that they were the only party that could effectively provide a strong opposition to the SNP and defend the Union. Their promise not to increase income tax was an attractive policy for many who had witnessed a drop in their pay packets through pay freezes and increases in pension contributions. The Conservatives had clearly outmanoeuvred Labour. In 2011 the Conservatives won only 15 seats; five years on it had more than doubled to 31 seats. In the regional list, the party gained 2 seats in Glasgow and 3 in Central, a remarkable turnaround.

For Labour, their electoral nightmare continued. The party which had once dominated Scottish politics was completely humiliated with the 'despised' Tories taking second place. In 1999, Labour won 56 seats, yet 17 years later that number had been reduced to just 24. In an election where polls indicated that 90 per cent of Yes voters would back the SNP, Labour had a straight battle with the Conservatives for the No voters. The Tory message was clear – total opposition to a second referendum and no tax rises. In contrast the Labour leader,

Kezia Dugdale, told an interviewer that it was 'not inconceivable' she could support independence if it would secure Scotland's membership of the European Union. Labour, through its promise to increase tax rates for basic earners by 1p, wished to place austerity issues at the heart of its campaign. However, the constitutional issues remained dominant. Labour's policy to make Scottish taxpayers pay more than their fellow UK citizens, persuaded some middle-class voters to switch to the Tories.

In terms of the minority parties, the Greens received six seats, pushing the Liberal Democrats into fifth spot. Yet while the combined constituency and list votes for the Liberal Democrats added up to just under 300,000, it was the Greens with a combined vote of about 160,000 who gained the most seats. So much for the fairness of the AMS system. The Liberal Democrats had at least retained their five seats and its leader, Willie Rennie, won a constituency seat (in contrast Kezia Dugdale failed to win her constituency seat). UKIP failed to make any impact and received only 2 per cent of the votes. Conversely, UKIP won 7 seats in Wales – their first – gaining 12.5 per cent of the votes.

National/regional party list

This PR system was introduced for elections to the European Parliament in England, Scotland and Wales (but not in Northern Ireland) in 1999. Here the electorate does not vote for individual party candidates but for a party. Political parties draw up a list of candidates in the order in which they will be elected. Representatives are elected from 11 large multi-member regions, each electing between 3 and 10 MEPs. In the 2014 European Election, Scotland elected 6 MEPs (see Tables 3.16 and 3.17).

In May 2014, the United Kingdom elected 72 MEPs (59 from England) to the European Parliament with Nigel Farage, the leader of UKIP, winning the most votes and seats. He declared the result 'an earthquake in British politics' and that UKIP was now 'a truly national force'.

The UKIP performance was impressive. UKIP increased its votes from the 2.49 million it had received in 2009 to 4.37 million. UKIP also topped the poll in six of the nine regions of England, with one of its strongest performances coming in the South-East where it doubled its MEPs to four. UKIP also increased its votes in Scotland and Wales. In Scotland, UKIP received 10.4 per cent of the votes, but more importantly it gained its first ever Scottish MEP and retained its Welsh seat.

Labour recovered from its poor showing of 2009 when only 11 of its MEPs were elected and narrowly beat the Conservatives to second place with 25.4 per cent of the national votes. Its best performance was in London where it increased its share of the vote from 21.7 per cent to 36.7 per cent.

The Conservative Party, which had been the largest UK party in the 2009 elections, lost support to UKIP. It lost 7 MEPs and was reduced to being the third largest party with 24 per cent of the votes. The then Conservative leader, David Cameron, claimed that the public was disillusioned with the EU. For the Liberal Democrats, it was another disastrous performance. Almost one million of their 2009 voters deserted the party resulting in it losing 10 of their 11 MEPs.

While Scotland followed some of the national trends, it had its own political dimension. The SNP once again had the most votes. It returned two MEPs, which was the same as in 2009. The Liberal Democrats lost their European seat and suffered a decline in votes. Labour retained its two seats with the Conservatives retaining their one seat and UKIP gaining one seat.

Advantages of the regional list

- There is greater proportionality between votes cast and seats gained. In the 2004 European Elections, which used FPTP, Labour gained 44 per cent of the vote and received 74 per cent of the seats.
- It rewards smaller parties. In the 2009 European Elections, UKIP won 16.5 per cent of the vote and received 13 seats (the same as Labour).

Disadvantages of the regional list

- The link between representatives and constituents is weakened in large multi-member constituencies. Very few people in Scotland could name their MEP.

Table 3.16 European Election results, 2014: Scotland

Party	Votes		MEPs (total)
	Total	%	
SNP	389,503	29.0	2
Labour	348,219	25.9	2
Conservative	231,330	17.2	1
Liberal Democrats	95,319	7.0	0
Green	108,305	8.6	0
UKIP	140,353	10.4	1

Table 3.17 European election results, 2014: Great Britain

Party	Votes		MEPs	
	Total	%	Total	+/−
UKIP	4,376,275	27.5	24	+11
Labour	4,020,646	25.4	20	+7
Conservative	3,792,549	23.9	19	−7
Green	1,255,573	7.9	3	+1
Liberal Democrats	1,087,633	6.9	1	−10

Seats: UK 72, Turnout: 15,625,823 (34.5%), Electorate: 45,315,669

Single transferable vote

This PR system was used in the Scottish local government elections for the first time in May 2007. It is also used in Northern Ireland for elections to both the Northern Ireland Assembly and the European Parliament.

The main features of STV are:

1 Representatives are chosen from multi-member constituencies. In a five-member local government constituency (ward), voters rank their preferences among the candidates using the figures 1–5. Often the number of candidates will be in double figures.
2 Electors can vote for as many or as few candidates as they like.
3 A complicated quota system is used to calculate the minimum number of votes required to win one of the seats. The quota is calculated by dividing the number of votes cast by the number of seats available plus one. In a four-member constituency where 150,000 votes were cast, a candidate would require 30,001 votes in order to be elected. Any votes in excess of this quota are redistributed on the basis of second preferences.

The Local Governance (Scotland) Act (2004) facilitated this change from the traditional FPTP system to a form of PR. It resulted in substantial change in both the composition and political control of Scottish local authorities.

Scottish local government elections 2007 and 2012

The introduction of the STV system in 2007 has led to a fairer distribution of seats among the parties. However, it is now more difficult for one party to gain overall control of a council and this means that most councils have a coalition administration. Labour dominance of local government has ended with Labour experiencing a significant reduction in its number of councillors. In 2003, Labour had 509 councillors and overall control of 13 councils. The SNP had 181 councillors and overall control of one council. In contrast, in the 2007 elections using STV, the SNP gained the most councillors, having 363 but control of no council, and Labour dropped to 348 councillors and control of two councils.

The 2012 local council elections further highlighted the fairness of STV. Both the SNP and Labour claimed that they were the winners in these elections. The SNP could argue that they had the most seats and the largest increase in the number of councillors, while Labour could argue that they controlled the most councils, including

Glasgow, which the SNP had hoped to win. The Liberal Democrats did very badly – they lost 95 seats and suffered the humiliation of an Independent candidate, dressed as a penguin, receiving more votes than the Liberal Democrat candidate in an Edinburgh ward.

Table 3.17 **2012 local council election results**

Party	Number of councillors	Net gain/loss compared with 2007 elections
Scottish National Party	425	+62
Scottish Labour	394	+46
Scottish Liberal Democrats	71	–95
Scottish Conservative	115	–28
Scottish Green	14	+6

Table 3.18 **Councils controlled by Labour, SNP, Independents**

Party	2003 (FPTP)	2007 (STV)	2012 (STV)
Labour	13	2	4
SNP	1	0	2
Independents	6	3	4
Total councils	20	5	10

Show your understanding

1 Describe briefly how AMS works in Scotland.
2 AMS ensures a fairer distribution of seats and a greater choice for the electorate. To what extent did the 2007 and 2011 Scottish Parliament elections achieve this outcome?
3 Describe how the national/regional party list system operates and its impact on the political parties in the 2009 and 2014 European elections.
4 Describe briefly how the STV system operates.
5 Outline the impact of STV on the Scottish local council elections of 2007 and 2012.

Developing your skills

To what extent were the 2011 and 2016 Scottish Parliament elections a triumph for the SNP and a disaster for all the other parties?

1 West Dunbartonshire
2 East Dunbartonshire
3 North Lanarkshire
4 Glasgow City
5 East Renfrewshire
6 Renfrewshire
7 Inverclyde
8 Clackmannanshire
9 Falkirk
10 West Lothian
11 City of Edinburgh
12 Midlothian

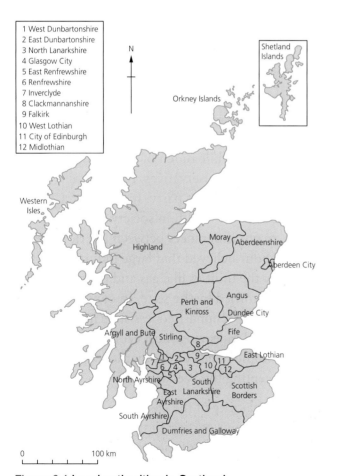

Figure 3.4 **Local authorities in Scotland**

The study of voting behaviour – the ways in which the public decide which political party to vote for – is a complex issue. Which party an individual votes for is influenced by long-term factors such as social class, age, ethnic and religious background and region; and by short-term factors such as governing competence, the state of the economy and the popularity of the respective parties' leaders and policies.

Political scientists have developed theories of voting behaviour to explain the interaction between the electorate and their voting preferences. They can be divided into long-term and short-term factors.

Long-term influences

The main theories are the sociological and party identification models, which focus on the social characteristics of voters – especially social class.

Short-term influences

The main theory is the rational choice model, which focuses on the significant factors pertaining to a particular issue. In the 2015 General Election, the competence of Ed Miliband, the handling of the economy and, in Scotland, the impact of the 2014 referendum were all key factors.

Long-term factors were considered to be the most important influence on voting behaviour in the period 1945–78. This was the era of party identification, class alignment and two-party

dominance. The period between 1979 and the present day is described as one of declining party identification and partisan de-alignment. Short-term factors such as the image of party leaders and the state of the economy are now considered to have a much greater influence on voting behaviour.

Class voting and partisanship

Until the late 1980s, social class was regarded as the dominant influence in voting behaviour. P.J. Pulzer, the Oxford political scientist, stated in 1967: 'Class is the basis of British party politics; all else is embellishment and detail.'

Most people voted for the party that best represented the interest of their social class. A large majority of the working class voted for the Labour Party, while much of the middle class supported the Conservatives. Ideologically, Labour was a socialist party. It stood for a redistribution of wealth in society in order to reduce major differences between the rich and poor. Labour believed that large industries, especially the utilities like gas and electricity, should be owned by the state. In contrast the Conservatives emphasised less state interference and believed in leaving most economic decision making in the hands of the market economy, while accepting the Welfare State.

The vast majority of the electorate voted for one of the two major parties: in the 1951 General Election 97 per cent of the electorate voted either Conservative or Labour. This continuity in voting patterns reflected long-term feelings of positive attachment to one of the main parties (partisanship). This distinct party identification, similar to attachment to a football club, was passed down from generation to generation.

However, both class voting and partisanship have declined since the 1970s. The 2015 election result in Scotland witnessed the complete collapse of class voting, with national identity becoming the dominant factor.

Party membership

The general trend of people being less strongly affiliated to parties is reflected in the decreasing number of party members:

- Conservative membership peaked at about 2.8 million members in the 1950s, but had fallen to 134,000 by 2014.
- In the same period Labour membership fell from about 1.1 million to 187,000.

- As a result of the Scottish referendum membership of the SNP surged from just under 26,000 to more than 100,000, making the SNP the UK's third largest party.
- The result of falling membership is a large and growing number of floating voters, especially the young, with falling turnout and no lasting loyalty to any party.

What is social class?

Social class is defined by social and economic status. The working class consists of people in manual occupations and the middle class comprises those in non-manual employment.

The market research definition of class structure uses six categories:

- Categories A, B and C1 are the non-manual middle class.
- Categories C2, D and E constitute the manual working class.

Figure 4.1 A category A worker

Figure 4.2 A category C2 worker

Partisan de-alignment

The changing trends in social class and voting have been explained by Professor Ivor Crewe (see Fact file). The result of his analysis can be seen in the decline in the number of voters who identified strongly with either Labour or the Conservatives. In 1961, 44 per cent of voters were 'very strong' supporters of one of the main parties, but by 2010 this figure had dropped to only 12 per cent. The core vote for the two main political parties has declined significantly, so parties now have to work harder to win over floating voters who do not have strong allegiances and switch their votes from election to election. This explains why in the 1980s the Conservatives gained support from the working class. In the 1974 General Election only 26 per cent of the skilled working class (C2) voted Conservative; in 1987, 40 per cent voted Conservative. The Conservative governments of the 1980s tapped into the aspirations of this new upwardly mobile, skilled working class through policies such as the sale of council houses, lower taxation and the opportunity for ordinary workers to buy shares in newly privatised industries such as gas and electricity.

New Labour, under the leadership of Tony Blair, was determined to modernise the Labour Party by ending its commitment to socialism. New Labour offered the 'third way' by appealing to the middle classes and becoming a catch-all party through low taxation, increased NHS spending and attractive social policies such as the introduction of the minimum wage. Labour retained its gains among middle class voters in 2001 and 2005 but its working class vote fell. When he became Conservative leader, David Cameron copied Tony Blair and modernised his party. This enabled the Conservatives to win both the 2010 and 2015 General Elections.

The 2015 election share of votes indicates that UKIPs main support came from classes C2, D

Fact file

The de-alignment explanation

De-alignment means a weakening relationship between social class and party support – a decline in the class basis of UK politics. Ivor Crewe argued that the distinction between social classes had been eroded by changes in the labour market (the decline of heavy industry), the increase in female workers, greater affluence and improved access to higher education. Crewe divided the working class into two groups: the old working class and the new working class, who aspire to be middle class.

Features of the old working class:
* unskilled manual occupation in traditional heavy industries
* trade union membership
* living in a council house
* located in greater numbers in the north of England, Wales and Scotland.

Features of the new working class:
* more likely to be skilled with better qualifications
* owner-occupiers, many having bought their council house under the Conservative policy of right to buy
* working in new high-tech industries
* found in greater number in the southern half of England.

In the 1987 General Election only 18 per cent of the middle classes voted Labour: in 1997, 34 per cent voted Labour. In 1997 only 27 per cent of C2 skilled working class voted Conservative: in 2010 the figure had risen to 37 per cent.

and E (see Table 4.2). A 2013 YouGov poll indicated that the top priority for working-class voters was reducing immigration – immigration control was one of the top policy aims of UKIP.

It should be emphasised that, despite the decline of class voting, it is still an important factor. Labour remains the most popular party among working-class voters and the Conservatives the most popular among the middle class. What is interesting is that semi/unskilled working-class voters in the south are more likely to vote Conservative than professionals and managers in the north, where voters of all classes have not forgotten the impact of Tory Thatcherism on northern industry. This suggests that geography is now more important than class.

Table 4.1 **Class voting, selected years (share of the vote, %), 2015 result refers to only England and Wales**

	Middle class (ABC1)	Skilled working class (C2)	Unskilled working class (DE)
Conservative			
1979	59	41	34
1997	39	27	21
2010	39	37	31
2015	43	32	27
Labour			
1979	24	41	49
1997	34	50	59
2010	27	29	40
2015	27	32	41

Table 4.2 **UKIP share of the vote (%) by social class England and Wales 2015**

Overall vote	Middle class (ABC1)	Skilled working class (C2)	Unskilled working class (DE)
12.6	9.5	19	17

Show your understanding

1 Outline the long-term and short-term influences on voting behaviour.
2 Outline the evidence that supports the view that social class was once regarded as being the most important factor in voting behaviour.
3 Refer to Table 4.1 and Table 4.2. What conclusions can be made regarding social class and party support?
4 Explain the term 'partisan de-alignment' and describe its impact on voting behaviour.

Geography/regional differences

There are clear regional variations in voting in Britain. A 'north–south' divide is evident, with Labour support highest in the north of England, Scotland (prior to the 2015 election), Wales, and large urban areas and council-house schemes; the Conservatives do best in southern England, and in English suburbs and rural areas. The geographical divisions in voting patterns in England and Wales can be explained in part by social class factors. Labour's safe seats tend to be in inner-city constituencies in cities such as Manchester and Liverpool. In contrast, Conservative safe seats tend to be in prosperous English constituencies in the suburbs and rural areas. The FPTP 2015 General Election as stated in Chapter 3 artificially divides the regions and nations of the UK. Labour continues to be under-represented in southern England – and now in Scotland; and the Conservatives likewise in the north. Labour won just eight seats out of 139 across the south-east and south-west of England despite winning about 1.3 million votes.

Table 4.3 Regional voting, 2015 General Election

	Conservative	Labour	Liberal Democrats
Overall			
Share of the vote (%)	36.9	30.4	7.9
Seats	331 (+35)	232 (–26)	8 (–49)
By region (share of the vote, %)			
North-East	25.3	46.9	6.5
Yorkshire and the Humber	32.6	39.1	7.1
North-West	31.2	44.6	6.5
West Midlands	41.8	32.9	5.5
East Midlands	43.4	31.6	5.6
London	34.9	43.7	7.7
South-East	50.8	18.3	9.3
South-West	46.5	17.7	15.1
Scotland	14.9	24.3	7.5
Wales	27.2	36.9	6.5

The end of social class voting in Scotland?

In the 2010 General Election, Labour had actually increased its votes and won back the two by-election seats it had lost during the 2005–10 Parliament. The political consensus even after the SNP victory in the Scottish Parliament elections was that in UK elections the Scottish electorate would remain loyal to Labour.

Prior to the 2014 Scottish independence referendum, the unionist parties expected an easy win as opinion polls suggested that only between a quarter and a third of Scots supported independence. Scottish Labour hoped that this would demoralise the SNP and their supporters, leading to Labour's dominance again in the 2015 General Election in Scotland. The reality was the opposite.

The referendum unleashed an exceptional level of public engagement and a surge in support for the SNP. Nationalism had replaced social class as the dominant voting factor in Scotland (in England and to a lesser extent in Wales, UKIP played a British/English national identity card with policies hostile to immigrants and to EU membership). Moreover Scottish Labour's alliance with the Conservatives in the Better Together campaign would have the same dire electoral effect experienced by the Scottish Liberal Democrats in the 2011 Scottish Parliament elections. It was Scottish Labour that experienced internal turmoil and demoralisation. Its leader, Johann Lamont, resigned in October 2014 claiming that the Scottish Labour Party was 'just a branch office of London'. In contrast the resignation of the SNP leader, Alex Salmond, led to the triumphant coronation of Nicola Sturgeon as party leader. Jim Murphy, a Scottish Labour MP, was elected leader of Scottish Labour.

The opinion polls suggested that the outcome of the election would be a hung parliament and this was to the advantage of SNP. Nicola Sturgeon, fighting on an anti-austerity platform, stated that the SNP would 'lock the Tories' out of power and offered to work with Ed Miliband in a progressive alliance.

Other social factors

Age

There are clear links between age and party support. In the last five elections in England and Wales, Labour outperformed the Conservatives among those aged 18–24 (42 per cent to 28 per cent). In contrast older groups have consistently favoured the Conservative Party; in age group 65+ the Conservative figure was 47 per cent compared to the Labour figure of 23 per cent (see Table 4.4). It should be noted that the growing number of elderly are more likely to vote than the young and this is advantageous to the Conservatives. In the 2015 General Election turnout for those under 25 was only 44 per cent; in contrast for those over 55 it was 78 per cent. The older generation were to play a key role in ensuring a 'Leave' vote in the 2016 EU Referendum.

Gender

Until the 1997 General Election women were more likely to vote Conservative than men. However, since then more women than men have voted Labour – although in both the 2010 and 2015 General Elections the gender vote favoured the Conservatives (see Table 4.5).

Similar to the general age pattern, young women under the age of 35 favoured Labour – 40 per cent to 30 per cent. In contrast older women favoured the Conservatives – in the 65+ group by a massive 47 per cent to 23 per cent. Given that in this age

group there are more women than men, this again is advantageous for the Conservatives.

Table 4.5 **Gender and voting, 2015 General Election**

	Conservative	Labour	Liberal Democrats
Men	38 (–)	30 (+2)	8 (–14)
Women	37(+1)	33 (+2)	8 (–16)

Ethnicity

Ethnic minority voters are traditionally far more likely to vote Labour and far less likely to vote Conservative. However, the impact of the Iraq War (short-term influence) contributed to a sharp drop of 5.5 per cent in support for Labour among Muslim voters in the 2005 General Election. During this election in Bethnal Green in London – a constituency with one of the largest Muslim electorates – George Galloway of the anti-war party Respect defeated the Labour candidate (however, at the 2010 General Election, Labour regained Bethnal Green). In the 2015 election two out of every three BME voters supported Labour. Given UKIPs anti-immigration policies, it received very little support from the BME community.

Table 4.4 **Age and voting (%), 2015 General Election**

	Conservative	Labour	Liberal Democrats
Overall			
Share of the vote (%)	36.9 (+0.8)	30.4 (+ 1.5)	7.9 (–15.2)
By age (share of the vote, %)			
18–24	28 (–2)	42 (+11)	5 (–26)
25–34	33 (–2)	36 (+6)	7 (–22)
35–44	35 (+1)	35 (+5)	10 (–16)
45–54	36 (+2)	33 (+5)	8 (–18)
55+	37 (–1)	31 (+3)	9 (–14)
65+	47 (+3)	23 (–8)	8 (–8)

Table 4.6 Vote by ethnic grouping (%), 2015 General Election

Group	Conservative	Labour	Liberal Democrats	UKIP
White	39	28	8	14
All BME	23	65	4	2

Fact file

Electoral turnout

The 2015 General Elections saw turnout increase slightly from 65 per cent to 66.1 per cent. However, it was still way below the post-war average of 78 per cent. Scotland experienced a much higher turnout of 71.1 per cent. This followed the huge upsurge in electoral registration and political engagement during the 2014 Scottish referendum and continued afterwards with a significant increase in SNP party membership.

Apathy and disillusionment

It is clear that there is growing dissatisfaction with the political parties and Westminster politics, which has led to a lower turnout. As stated, the proportion of the public who have a strong attachment to a political party has declined (although membership of the SNP and Labour under its new leader, Jeremy Corbyn, has increased). The 2009–10 MPs expenses scandal further eroded public confidence and created greater disillusionment. The Electoral Reform Society describes FPTP as 'a voting system in crisis' and stated that 'nearly half a million people signed petitions calling for electoral reform in the fortnight after the 2015 election'.

Social groupings

Clearly social factors influence turnout. Middle-class, university-educated individuals, older people and those living in rural areas are most likely to vote. People aged over 60 are almost twice as likely to vote as those aged 18–24.

Show your understanding

1 To what extent is there a 'north–south divide' in voting behaviour? You should also refer to Table 4.3 in your answer.
2 Why can it be argued that the 2015 General Election in Scotland marked the end of social class voting in Scotland?
3 Assess the other long-term influences on voting behaviour. You should refer to age, gender and race.

Short-term influences

The rational choice model considers the impact of short-term factors that influence the choice made by individual voters at elections. With the decline in party identification there is a growing number of floating voters who are undecided prior to a general election. They will be influenced by a range of issues such as the policies of the parties, the image of the party leader, the state of the economy and even by which newspaper they read.

Issue voting

All political parties outline their vision for the future and the policies to improve the quality of life of the electorate and their families (see extracts from the 2015 UK party manifestos on pages 55–56).

In the 2005 General Election Labour was still ahead on the major issues such as running the economy; this ensured a return to power, albeit with a reduced majority. Prime Minister Blair's popularity had declined as a result of British involvement in Iraq and the failure to find weapons of mass destruction there, contrary to Tony Blair's claims.

The 2010 General Election

The 2010 General Election centred round the state of the economy. The banking crisis of 2008 and its impact on the world and UK economy dominated the election. The age of prosperity had now gone and Britain faced a massive debt crisis which would lead to severe cuts in public expenditure. The age of austerity had arrived.

The Conservative strategy was to convince the electorate that another five years of a Labour Government would be a disaster for the UK. Supported by the Tory press David Cameron concentrated on the supposed weaknesses of Gordon Brown and the divisions within the Labour Party. Opinion polls clearly identified Cameron as having the best personality of the three leaders and having the best understanding of the problems facing Britain.

Cameron had neutralised the negative image that his party had had in previous elections (except in Scotland) but he failed to 'seal the deal' with the electorate. The Conservatives won the 2010 election but failed to achieve an overall majority; the outcome was a coalition government with the Liberal Democrats. Five years later the Liberal Democrats' decision to form a government with the Conservatives would lead to electoral annihilation in a UK general election.

The 2015 General Election

Once again the handling of the economy and the personality of the Labour leader, Ed Miliband, would be the key campaign issues. Immigration and membership of the European Union (EU) were the key policy issues for UKIP and its supporters. In a Lord Ashcroft poll carried out in May 2015, 87 per cent of UKIP voters regarded immigration as one of the three most important issues facing the country. (In the 2014 European election UKIP achieved a historic victory by winning the most votes and seats.) Two Conservative MPs switched to UKIP and the concern for David Cameron was that Conservative supporters hostile to the EU might switch to UKIP. This explains why the Conservatives included in their manifesto a promise to hold a referendum on UK membership of the EU.

The Conservatives promised to continue with significant cuts to public expenditure, while Labour would cut the budget deficit much less deeply than David Cameron. The Conservatives highlighted that the economy was now the fastest growing among EU countries.

Table 4.7 indicates the link between people's perception of the economy and their voting preference. The prosperous south (excluding parts of London) had fewer public sector workers and people on benefits. The massive shedding of public sector posts and cuts to welfare made by the Coalition Government impacted most on Scotland, the north of England and Wales. However, Labour had to compete with UKIP, the Green Party and the SNP for the votes of those unhappy with the state of the economy.

The poll also highlighted the public's perception of the party leaders. What was clear was that David Cameron was more popular than his party; in contrast the Labour Party was more popular than its leader Ed Miliband. (Around 79 per cent of Conservative voters had the competence of David Cameron as one of the three main reasons for their choice. In contrast only 39 per cent of Labour voters had.)

The YouGov poll makes interesting reading; the electorate were not convinced that either party would improve their family finances. However, there was a 9 per cent gap in favour of the Conservatives in terms of whether Britain as a whole would be better off (see Figure 4.3).

Table 4.7 **Vote choice by economic perception 2015**

Vote choice	Already feeling benefit (%)	Do not expect to feel benefit (%)
Conservative	64	10
Labour	12	32

Source: The Ashcroft Poll, May 2015

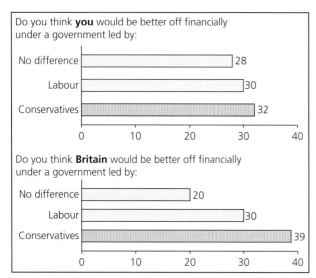

Figure 4.3 **Family finance perception**
Source: YouGov, 2015

The threat from the north

Opinion polls predicted a hung parliament and the possibility of the SNP being the 'King-makers'; Conservatives played on this fear among English voters by campaigning on a negative platform that a vote for Labour would make Alex Salmond the puppet-master. Conservative election billboards used this theme (see Figure 4.4).

The former Conservative Prime Minister, John Major, demanded that Ed Miliband rule out any pact with the SNP. Instead of concentrating on policy issues, the Labour leader was eventually forced to publicly state that no pact would be formed. This happened shortly before the election, but the damage had been done. Ironically the opinion polls were wrong. Flawed methodology had been used; the danger of a hung parliament was the creation of the polls and the media, and Labour suffered. Opinion polls had distorted and hijacked the real key policy issues.

Figure 4.4 **Conservative billboard showing Ed Miliband in the pocket of Alex Salmond**

Impact of referenda

A referendum is a ballot in which the voters, not their representatives in parliament, pass judgement on a particular issue. They are not held often in Britain but are common in other countries such as the USA. It is a form of direct democracy because it involves citizens directly in decision making. A referendum can be useful for overcoming divisions within a government.

Three national referenda have been held; one in 1975 on continued membership of the European Union, a second on the same in 2016, and one in 2011 on the introduction of the AV voting system (see page 36). Referenda have also been held to establish a devolved government in Scotland and a devolved assembly in Wales. In November 2004, a resounding 'No' vote ended Labour's plan for a regional assembly in the north-east of England.

Opponents of referenda argue that it undermines the UK system of representative democracy, undermines parliamentary sovereignty and can enable pressure groups to influence the outcome. Some would say that the 2016 EU Referendum is a case in point.

The result of past referenda or the potential threat of a future referendum has played an important role in the voting choices of some electorate.

The Scottish independence referendum 'No' vote energised the SNP as frustrated 'Yes' voters joined the party in record numbers. Scottish Labour also suffered from its alliance with the Conservative Party in the Better Together referendum campaign.

The referendum on membership of the EU promised by David Cameron in the Conservative manifesto significantly reduced the threat from UKIP. Many right-wing Conservative voters who voted UKIP in the 2014 European elections returned to the Conservative fold. This enabled the Conservatives to take Liberal Democrat seats in the south of England and thus gain an overall majority.

Main policies of the political parties at the 2015 General Election

Conservative

Main pledges

- Eliminate the deficit and be running a surplus by the end of the parliament
- Extra £8 billion above inflation for the NHS by 2020
- Extend Right to Buy to housing association tenants in England
- Legislate so that people working 30 hours on minimum wage pay no income tax
- Provide 30 hours of free childcare per week for working parents of 3- and 4-year-olds
- Have a referendum on Britain's EU membership
- Would 'honour in full our commitments to Scotland' and introduce 'English votes for English laws'
- Repeal the Human Rights Act and introduce a British bill of rights

Labour

Main pledges

- Responsibility 'triple lock': fully funded manifesto, cut the deficit every year, balance the books as soon as possible in next parliament
- Extra £2.5 billion for NHS, largely paid for by a mansion tax on properties valued at over £2 million
- Raise minimum wage to more than £8 per hour by 2019
- No rise in VAT, NI or basic and higher rates of income tax
- Access to childcare from 8am to 6pm for parents of primary school children
- Freeze energy bills until 2017 and give energy regulator new powers to cut bills this winter
- 'Home Rule Bill' to give extra powers to Scotland as agreed by Smith Commission and pass an English Devolution Act
- Reduce voting age to 16 and retain Human Rights Act

Liberal Democrats

Main pledges

- Balance the budget fairly through a mixture of cuts and taxes on higher earners
- Increase tax-free allowance to £12,500
- Guarantee education funding from nursery to age 19 with an extra £2.5 billion and qualified teachers in every class
- Invest £8 billion in the NHS, with equal care for mental and physical health
- Five new laws to protect nature and fight climate change
- Extra powers to Scotland as agreed by Smith Commission and introduce an English-only stage in the legislative process
- Reduce voting age to 16 and retain Human Rights Act

UKIP

Main pledges

- Have a rapid referendum on Britain's membership of the EU
- Control immigration with points system, limit of 50,000 skilled workers a year and a five-year ban on unskilled immigrants
- Extra £3 billion a year for the NHS in England
- No tax on the minimum wage
- Meet NATO target of spending 2 per cent of GDP on defence, and look to increase it 'substantially'
- English-only votes in Westminster and reduce the Barnett formula
- Introduce proportional representation

SNP

Main pledges

- Spending increase of 0.5 per cent a year, enabling £140 billion of extra investment
- Annual UK target of 100,000 affordable homes
- Increase in minimum wage to £8.70 by 2020
- Restore the 50p top income tax rate for those earning more than £150,000; introduce a mansion tax and a bankers' bonus tax
- Build an alliance against the renewal of Trident
- Retain the triple lock on pensions and protect the winter fuel allowance. At present, all pensioners receive an income rise of 2.5% or higher, depending on the rate of inflation.
- Implementation of Smith Commission and abolish House of Lords
- Introduce PR system of voting – single transferable vote

The media and elections

The role of the media in decision making in government is discussed in Chapter 8 and in this section we will concentrate only on its influence on the 2010 and 2015 elections (see pages 21–22 for influence of media in the Scottish 2014 Referendum).

A distinction is now made between the old media (television and newspapers) and the new media of social networking sites such as Facebook and Twitter. It was expected that the new media would dominate the 2010 UK General Election, yet it was the old media that shaped and transformed the campaigning process. The televised debates between the three leaders made television king and provided Nick Clegg, Liberal Democrat leader, with the opportunity to undermine the dominance of the two-party system.

Televised debates 2010

- First ever televised debates (three in all) between the three party leaders
- The first debate was a triumph for Nick Clegg and in the opinion polls the Liberal Democrat share of votes had risen by over 10 points. However, this surge in support was not reflected in the actual voting
- Viewing figure for first debate was 9.9 million
- Tory press character-assassinated Nick Clegg after the debates (Gordon Brown was obviously also a target). Journalist Nicholas Jones wrote: 'In the final stages of the election campaign, the fawning of the Tory press in their coverage of Cameron was matched only by the brutality of their treatment of Gordon Brown and their savage character assassination of Clegg.'

The impact of new media

Once again it was expected that the 2015 General Election would be dominated by the new media. In 2010 only one in three individuals belonged to a social network, by 2015 it was more than half of the population. It was estimated that there were about 7 million tweets to politicians during the 10 weeks leading up to the elections. The public could sign up for Twitter updates from the parties and individual politicians. Social media may put people in contact with more political opinions than their own, compared to newspapers.

However, its influence should not be overestimated as social media remains largely the domain of young people who are less likely to vote. Again during the Scottish 2014 Referendum more than 80 per cent of tweets were supportive of the 'Yes' campaign, but this was not reflected in the actual voting.

The role of television

Unlike newspapers, television channels are expected not to favour a particular political party and instead to display balance.

Once again a televised debate was eventually held. David Cameron, despite demanding a televised debate in 2010 between the three main party leaders, refused to sanction a 'rematch'. He only agreed to a seven-way debate which included other party leaders such as Nicola Sturgeon and Natalie Bennett of the Greens. This main televised debate did not achieve the same overall coverage and interest as the 2010 debates.

Figure 4.5 **The election candidates who took part in the 2015 televised debates**

According to a survey by Panelbase, 62 per cent of the public agreed that television was 'by far the most influential media source' in providing information about the 2015 General Election. Significantly 38 per cent stated that the coverage of the leadership debate had helped to shape their views.

Table 4.6 **Newspaper readership and party affiliation, 2015 General Election (%)**

Newspaper	Conservative	Labour	Liberal Democrat	UKIP
Mirror	11	67	5	9
Guardian	6	62	11	1
Independent	17	47	16	4
Sun	47	24	4	19
Times	55	20	13	6
Mail	59	14	5	19
Telegraph	69	8	8	12

Source: Based on a survey of 100,000 GB adults–You Gov/General Election 2015

Television (and newspaper) debate reflected the key issues of the campaign. The consensus of the opinion polls was that Labour and Conservatives were neck and neck and this became the dominant issue in the week leading up to voting. Ed Miliband on BBC *Question Time*, under severe media pressure, ruled out any possibility of a Labour/SNP coalition (see page 54).

Do newspapers influence the outcome of elections?

Influence of the media

Ever since the *Sun*'s 1992 notorious front-page headline 'It's the Sun wot won it', claiming credit for the Conservatives' victory, there has been an ongoing debate between academics and political strategists about the extent to which any one paper can influence voters. Yes, there is a correlation between newspapers read by an individual and their party affiliation as indicated in Table 4.6. However, Tory supporters are aware for example that the *Daily Mail* supports the Conservative Party and they buy it as it reflects their views.

John Curtice, professor of politics at Strathclyde University, argues that there is no evidence to support the view that newspaper endorsement affects elections and that the 'aggregate effect of newspapers' influence approximates to zero'. The Scottish Parliament elections are a case in point. In 2007 the two best-selling newspapers in Scotland, the *Daily Record* and the *Sun*, supported Labour and were hostile to the SNP yet the SNP won the election and formed a minority government. An alternative argument might be that if these newspapers had supported the SNP (as the *Sun* did in 2011 and 2016), then the SNP might have had a greater number of MSPs.

What is clear is that politicians and their spin doctors dearly wish to have the support of the best-selling newspapers. Neil Kinnock, the former Labour leader, is convinced to this day that the *Sun*'s vicious anti-Labour campaign enabled the Conservatives to win the 1992 election. Martin Linton, author of *Was It the Sun Wot Won It?*, argues that 'The *Sun*'s readers are less committed to a party, less interested in politics, so more easily influenced by attacks on character and distortion'.

Up to 1997 the British press was predominantly Conservative in its political support. New Labour under Blair shook off its socialist beliefs and entered the 1997 election as a united party: in contrast, the Tories were divided. Blair's meetings with Rupert Murdoch paid off, and in 1997 the *Sun* switched to Labour, claiming it was the natural party of government. Murdoch's News International continued to support Labour in the 2001 and 2005 elections. However, in 2010 and again in 2015 it supported the Conservatives. (In Scotland the *Sun* supported the SNP.)

The majority of newspapers support the Conservatives; the right-wing press has a much larger readership than the left-wing press. During the election, the combined readership of the *Daily Mail*, the *Sun* and *Telegraph* was just under four million compared to just over one million for the *Guardian* and *Daily Mirror*.

The media's concentration on a possible Labour/SNP coalition did no harm to the Tory cause. The *Daily Mail* on 6 May devoted its front page and three further pages on the constitutional nightmare of a Labour/SNP alliance. The *Mail* stated that such an arrangement would 'destroy our economy and our very nation'. What is clear is that all of the media, by believing erroneous polls, boosted Conservative support – just ask Nick Clegg (he resigned as Liberal Democrat leader after the election).

Show your understanding

1. Outline the main issues and influences on voters in the 2015 General Election.
2. What evidence suggests that newspapers influence voting behaviour?
3. Why do television channels and radio stations aim to provide balanced coverage of elections?
4. Assess the impact of the televised debates on the outcome of the 2010 and 2015 General Elections.
5. Refer to Table 4.6 and pages 57–59. What evidence is there to suggest that newspapers are more likely to support the Conservative Party?
6. Outline the arguments for and against referenda.

12-mark questions

1. 'Some factors are more important in influencing voting behaviour than others.'
   Evaluate the importance of a range of factors that influence voting behaviour. You should refer to recent elections held in Scotland or the United Kingdom or both in your answer.
2. Evaluate the influence of social class on voting behaviour.

20-mark question

To what extent is the media the most important influence on voting behaviour? You should refer to voting behaviour in Scotland or the United Kingdom or both in your answer.

The first elections to the Scottish Parliament were held on 6 May 1999 when 129 new Members of the Scottish Parliament (MSPs) were elected to represent and serve the people of Scotland. They make the decisions that shape our country and work to better the lives of their constituents. Each of the 129 MSPs represents a particular area of the country known as a constituency or a region. Of the 129 MSPs, 73 represent a constituency and 56 represent 8 regions of Scotland (there are 7 MSPs in each region).

The role of political representatives

The basic role of an MSP does not significantly differ to that of an MP. As well as their party allegiance, each MSP must work for the Scottish Parliament and for their constituency or region. The nature of the role demands juggling a complex set of responsibilities and MSPs will essentially have two workplaces. They will perform work in parliament but also in their constituency with time being split between the two. Further to this, if an MSP is part of the Scottish Government then he or she may also have ministerial responsibilities as well. On the other hand, if an MSP is not part of the government or shadow cabinet then a huge part of their job as political representatives is to hold the government to account and to scrutinise their work. These MSPs are often referred to as backbench MSPs.

Work of an MSP inside parliament

- MSPs ask government ministers questions on behalf of their constituents or other interests. These can be written questions and or posed questions in the Scottish Parliament (see parliamentary questions on the next page).
- Much of an MSP's time in the chamber is spent debating the key issues affecting the country and on legislation that may be passing through parliament.
- As a member of a committee, MSPs will have a number of duties to carry out including scrutinising legislation and conducting inquiries.
- MSPs also have the power to attempt to introduce new Bills (laws). They are allowed to attempt to introduce two new Bills during one parliamentary session.
- MSPs will vote on legislation during Decision Time. All MSPs have one vote each and so at this time all MSPs, in theory, have equal power.

Work of an MSP outside parliament

- MSPs will often meet with a wide variety of people in their local constituencies. Councillors, local organisations and local pressure groups would all look to meet with MSPs, hoping that any issues they have could possibly be raised at the highest levels of government.
- MSPs will be expected to spend some of their time attending various events in their constituency, for example, the opening of a new business or an awards ceremony.
- In order to keep a good profile within their constituency, MSPs will often appear in local newspapers or on local TV and radio. Social media is also a very important form of communication (see page 132).

MSPs will hold a weekly surgery so constituents can come and seek advice or make a complaint or suggestion about a local or national issue.

Parliamentary questions

Parliamentary questions are one of the key ways in which individual MSPs can hold the government to account and extract information relating to policies and decisions. There are different ways MSPs can ask questions in the Scottish Parliament.

First Minister's Question Time

Every Thursday for up to 45 minutes, MSPs can ask questions of the first minister in the chamber. Opposition leaders will ask questions which will be followed by questions from backbench MSPs. Opposition MSPs will aim to ask difficult and demanding questions of the first minister in the hope of catching her out and damaging the reputation of the current government. For example, after the publication of the Scottish Survey of Literacy and Numeracy highlighted a drop in attainment in Scottish schools, opposition leaders forced Nicola Sturgeon into admitting numeracy results were 'unacceptable'. This admission made the evening news and was in every newspaper the following day, putting the government under intense pressure and shining the spotlight on the government's education policy. Parliament also gets the opportunity to question ministers and cabinet secretaries during **General Question Time** and **Topical Question Time**.

Representation

As much as women have come to dominate positions of political leadership in Scotland, the results of the 2016 Election were disappointing. Only 45 women MSPs (34.9 per cent) were elected to the fifth Scottish Parliament, the exact same proportion as in 2011. Thus, despite optimistic predictions, the 2003 Scottish Parliament election remains the high point of women's representation in Scotland at all political levels (at 39.5 per cent). It is difficult to explain the result. In the run-up to the 2016 Scottish Parliament election, candidate selection trends were promising. All of the parties (except the Conservatives) saw improvements in their share of women candidates from 2011.

In the case of the SNP, over 40 per cent of their constituency and list candidates were women, an increase that reflects the party's implementation (for the first time) of gender quotas in the form of all-women shortlists (AWS) in constituencies with retiring SNP MSPs. These measures had a clear impact – 43 per cent of SNP MSPs elected in 2016 were women (compared to 27.5 per cent in 2011). Eight of the nine SNP women selected under AWS were elected, and a number of new faces have entered the Scottish Parliament for the first time.

Turning to Scottish Labour, 46 per cent of the party's MSPs in 2016 were women (the same proportion as in 2011). While over 50 per cent of the party's constituency candidates were women (in part due to the use of AWS), Labour's poor electoral performance meant that they only held on to three constituencies – including Jackie Baillie's Dumbarton seat. However, the party's use of gender quotas on the list – in the form of 'zipping', or alternating, male and female candidates – meant that almost half of their list MSPs elected were women (48 per cent).

Yet while the SNP and Labour's use of quotas has made a difference, the overall figures have stagnated due in large part to an unexpectedly strong Tory performance across Scotland. Only around 19 per cent of Scottish Conservative candidates were women, and one of their

Table 5.1 **Scottish Parliament 2016 by party and gender**

Party	Female	Male	Total	% Female
SNP	27	36	63	42.9
Conservative	6	25	31	19.4
Labour	11	13	24	45.8
Green	1	5	6	16.7
Liberal Democrat	0	5	5	0
Total	35	84	129	34.9

regional lists, Highlands and Islands, was men only. Top list places were also predominantly taken by men, with the party's North East Scotland list returning four male MSPs, while West Scotland included more candidates named 'Maurice' (two, both elected), than it did women (one, in tenth position). The same number of Conservative women were elected as in 2011 – six – but this is set in the context of the party more than doubling its seats, which means that only 19 per cent of Conservative MSPs are women. The Liberal Democrats, as predicted, returned no women. The parliamentary party is now men only at both Holyrood and Westminster. The Greens, meanwhile, did 'zip' their regional list candidates and 50 per cent of their lists were topped by women. However, some unexpected wins and losses for the party meant that in the end, only one of six Green MSPs was a woman (17 per cent).

In terms of ethnicity, the Scottish Parliament still has only two black and minority ethnic (BME) MSPs – SNP Minister Humza Yousaf, who defeated Johann Lamont in Glasgow Pollok, and former Labour MP Anas Sarwar for the Glasgow region. This is disappointing as 4 per cent of the Scottish population are BME. Furthermore, it is concerning that there has never been a BME female MSP in the Scottish Parliament.

Show your understanding

1 Summarise the main tasks that MSPs undertake in parliament.
2 Summarise the main tasks that MSPs undertake in the constituency.
3 Compare the gender representation of the 2016 result with previous Scottish elections.
4 What did political parties do to try and increase female representation?
5 Which party was most successful in getting women elected?
6 Why is representation of ethnic minorities also disappointing?
7 'The Scottish Parliament is not accurately representative of the general population but is making improvements.' Is this statement true or false? Justify your answer.

ICT task

In groups of three, create a PowerPoint presentation investigating the role of MSPs in scrutinising the work of the Scottish Government. You will also need to refer to the section on committees (pages 70–73).

Pressures on representatives

Like MPs, MSPs are public servants who are first and foremost elected to serve their constituents. However, they will also be a member of a political party and must ensure they support the party's policies. This can often cause conflict, especially when the MSP has to balance these pressures with their own personal beliefs and opinions.

Party loyalty

See pages 87–89 for further discussion surrounding party limitations on representatives, including the whip system.

MSP rebellions

Sometimes an MSP may disagree with the direction their party or party leader is going with a certain policy. This can be serious enough to result in the MSP rebelling against the party whip and voting against a particular policy. If the policy is a 'red line issue' an MSP may feel completely at odds with their party's stance and decide to resign their party membership (see the case study on party loyalty versus personal beliefs).

Lobbying

Lobbying is a controversial but important part of democratic politics. MSPs who are in power and in place to make decisions will be targeted by lobbyists (usually corporate businesses, industry bodies, think tanks, law firms, management consultants and well-funded charities) whose paid job it is to influence the decisions taken by MSPs. Wherever there are politicians with the power to make decisions, there are lobbyists trying to influence those decisions. As the Scottish Parliament gets more powers, lobbying will increase. When the Scottish Government passed the minimum unit pricing on alcohol bill it faced a ferocious barrage of lobbying from the drinks industry including from the Scotch Whisky Association. The SWA has challenged the

Case study: Party loyalty versus personal beliefs – the SNP and NATO

One of the most famous Scottish political rebellions in recent years came in the run-up to the independence referendum when the SNP decided that, should Scotland ever become independent, then the country would apply to join NATO. This resulted in two SNP MSPs resigning in protest. John Finnie and Jean Urquhart, both MSPs in the Highlands, quit after the party very narrowly voted to overturn the decades-long ban on NATO membership. The MSPs insisted it was hypocritical and probably unworkable for the party to support the idea of Scotland joining a nuclear-armed military alliance while at the same time demanding that the UK removes the Trident nuclear weapons system from its base on the Clyde. John Finnie said, 'I cannot belong to a party that quite rightly does not wish to hold nuclear weapons on its soil, but wants to join a first-strike nuclear alliance. Although I envisage that I will continue to share common ground with the SNP on many issues, I cannot in good conscience continue to work as an SNP MSP.' Jean Urquhart, a Campaign for Nuclear Disarmament member for 35 years, said, 'The issue of nuclear disarmament and removing Trident from Scotland's waters is a red-line issue for me, and I could not remain committed to a party that has committed itself to retaining membership of NATO.'

legislation all the way to the European Court of Justice. Some argue that lobbying, especially by corporations, is controversial as it detracts from egalitarianism and promotes privileged access and corruption.

As the Scottish Parliament regards itself as a modern democratic parliament, in 2016 it passed the Lobbying (Scotland) Bill which creates a register of contacts who are paid to lobby MSPs in face-to-face meetings, events and hospitality occasions. Lobbyists are now required to register if they have met, or intend to meet, MSPs and are required to submit six-monthly returns of lobbying activity.

Tension between constituency and regional MSPs

Owing to the workings of the Additional Member System the traditional link between constituents and their representatives is now more complex. The constituency MSP represents a specific area and, having defeated other party candidates in a straightforward first past the post contest, he or she can claim to be the 'people's choice'. In the 2016 election George Adam SNP was elected as the constituency MSP for Paisley. However, voters in Paisley are also represented by seven regional MSPs. Both constituency and regional MSPs complain about each other's actions. Constituency MSPs are convinced that regional MSPs 'cherry pick' local issues and conduct electioneering with the purpose of winning the seat at a future election. In contrast, regional MSPs argue that constituency MSPs regard them as second-class politicians. It is significant that much of the criticism of regional MSPs now comes from SNP MSPs. SNP tends to do better in first past the post constituency elections and resents regional MSPs who failed to win under first past the post.

Show your understanding

1 Explain why party loyalty can sometimes be compromised. Refer to the case study in your answer.
2 a) What is lobbying?
  b) Why is lobbying controversial?
  c) What has the Scottish Parliament done to make lobbying more transparent?
3 Explain why there may be tension between constituency and regional MSPs.

12-mark question
Analyse the pressures facing political representatives.

The Legislature and Executive in Scotland

Background

Almost 300 years since the Act of Union dissolved the Scottish Parliament, a referendum was held on proposals for a directly elected Scottish Parliament with wide legislative powers. On 11 September 1997, these proposals received overwhelming support from the people of Scotland. The turnout was 60.4 per cent, with 74.3 per cent voting in favour of a Scottish Parliament and 60.2 per cent for the parliament to have tax-varying powers. This result was enough for Prime Minister Tony Blair to say, 'This is a good day for Scotland, and a good day for Britain and the United Kingdom … the era of big centralised government is over.' The following year, the Scotland Act (1998) cleared a pathway for the creation once again of a Scottish Parliament with the power to pass laws affecting Scotland in a variety of areas, known as devolved matters, which have been extended over the years (see Chapter 2).

Figure 5.1 **The Scottish Parliament**

Devolution

Devolution is the transfer or delegation of powers to a lower level, especially by central government to a local or regional administration. In the UK, some powers have been transferred from the UK Parliament at Westminster to various nations and regions. For example, different powers have been devolved to the Scottish Parliament, the National Assembly for Wales and the Northern Ireland Assembly. There are also levels of devolution in London and northern cities such as Manchester, which has control over its own health budget as well as having its own mayor. The UK now has three Executives, with devolved powers for 16.4 per cent of the population and one government for England and the UK (see Chapters 1 and 2 for full overview of constitutional arrangements).

The functions of the Scottish Parliament

The Scottish Parliament has four founding principles that aim to create an effective and accountable parliament, answering the needs of the people of Scotland. The four principles are: sharing power, accountability, openness and participation and equal opportunities. In achieving the four founding principles, the

Scottish Parliament regards itself as a model of modern democracy. For example, the Scottish Parliament should embody and reflect the sharing of power between the people of Scotland, the legislators and the Scottish Government. Furthermore, the Scottish Parliament should be accessible, open and responsive; it should develop procedures that make possible a participative approach to the development, consideration and scrutiny of policy and legislation.

The difference between the Scottish Parliament and the Scottish Government

The Scottish Parliament comprises all 129 elected Members of the Scottish Parliament (MSPs) and is the law-making body for devolved matters. It considers proposed legislation and scrutinises the activities and policies of the Scottish Government through debates, parliamentary questions and the work of committees.

The Scottish Government is the government in Scotland for devolved matters and, as such, it is responsible for defining and implementing policy in these areas. It is headed by the first minister and is made up of those MSPs who have been appointed by the first minister as Cabinet secretaries and ministers.

The Legislative process

A major role of any parliament is to make laws. The Scottish Parliament, in line with its founding principles, involves the whole people of Scotland along with regional and interested organisations, pressure groups and individuals, ensuring a high degree of accessibility and openness. This allows for a level of participation and the sharing of power that helps avoid a situation where the government can dominate the legislative process completely. Provision is made for individual MSPs and committees as well as the Executive to introduce or propose legislation. In effect, this provides a realistic opportunity for the people of Scotland to influence new laws with the aim of being a people's parliament by the sharing of power between the people of Scotland, the legislators and the Scottish Government.

> Before they become Acts of the Scottish Parliament, legislative proposals are known as bills. A bill becomes an Act by being passed by the parliament and receiving royal assent.

Pre-legislative consultation

Before any legislative proposal becomes a bill it goes through a pre-legislative consultation process. This whole process is designed to allow for maximum participation in an open and accessible manner. For example, with an executive bill the relevant minister informs the relevant committee of the proposed legislation and recommends which relevant groups or individuals should be involved in the pre-legislative consultation process. The Executive then consults the relevant bodies, identifying any issues of concern. In addition, the relevant committee is kept informed throughout. When the process is completed and the draft bill is introduced, the outcome of the consultation process is attached to it as a memorandum, ensuring openness from the start.

Types of bill

There are two different types of bill that can be introduced: a public bill and a private bill. All public bills are introduced by MSPs in the parliament. They may be introduced by members of the Scottish Government as an executive bill (sometimes referred to as a government bill), by one of the parliament's committees as a committee bill or by an individual MSP as a members' bill. A private bill can be introduced by an individual or group of people.

The majority of bills introduced and passed are executive bills. This is because the government can usually rely on their MSPs to support legislation. Most parties use a 'whip system' to ensure party unity in voting.

Executive bills

These are bills introduced by a Scottish Government cabinet secretary or minister, and they account for the majority of legislation passed by the Scottish Parliament. A few examples of executive bills include the Human Trafficking and Exploitation (Scotland) Act and the Air Weapons and Licensing (Scotland) Act.

Committee bills

A committee bill is a public bill introduced by the Convener of a committee of the Scottish Parliament to carry out a proposal made by the committee for a bill in relation to matters within its remit. The proposal is made by way of a report to the parliament. The bill cannot be introduced if the Scottish Government or the UK Government has indicated that they are planning to introduce legislation to give effect to the proposal. Between 2011 and 2016, only one committee bill was introduced; it successfully passed and received royal assent.

When the first committee bill was passed by the parliament, Alasdair Morgan MSP, then convener of the Justice Committee, said: 'The ability of Scottish Parliament committees to initiate legislation is an important part of what makes our system of governance innovative and fundamentally different from Westminster.'

Community Charge Debt (Scotland) Bill 2015

Introduced by: John Swinney MSP

Purpose and objectives of the bill: the intention of the bill was to end collection of community charge (more commonly known as 'poll tax') debts.

Passage of the bill

The Community Charge Debt (Scotland) Bill was introduced in Parliament on 3 December 2014. The Finance Committee was designated as the lead committee on the bill and the timetable for the bill was short. The Finance Committee took Stage 1 oral evidence on the general principles of the bill on 14 January 2015. The Stage 1 debate took place on 29 January 2015. Stage 2 consideration took place on 4 February 2015, and the bill was passed at Stage 3 on 19 February 2015 following a final debate. The bill received royal assent on 25 March 2015.

Members' bills

Individual MSPs, who are not members of the Scottish Government, can also introduce public bills. These are termed 'members' bills'. Each MSP can introduce a maximum of two members' bills in a session. An MSP introducing a member's bill must first lodge a draft proposal giving the short title of the proposed bill and an explanation of its purpose or intention. A member's bill must receive support from at least 18 MSPs representing at least half of the political parties (or groups) with five or more members in the parliament.

Between 2011 and 2016, six members' bills received royal assent.

Private bills

Private bills differ slightly from public bills and are subject to different procedures. A private bill is introduced by what is known as a promoter. A promoter can be an individual person, a group of people or a company; therefore, these are sometimes known as 'personal bills'. Generally they relate to development projects or changes to the use of land rather than changes to national laws.

There were only five successful private bills from 2011 to 2016.

The most well-known private bill was the Glasgow Airport rail link bill, which gave powers to the Strathclyde Passenger Transport Executive to construct a new railway service between Glasgow Airport and Glasgow Central Station. Unfortunately, the SNP Government cancelled the project as a result of the recession.

Legislation and the UK Supreme Court

After a bill is passed by the Scottish Parliament a period of four weeks must elapse before the Presiding Officer can submit it for royal assent. During this period the bill may be referred to the

Table 5.2 **All bills considered by the Scottish Parliament in session 4 (2011–16)**

Legislation	Government	Members'	Private	Committee	Total
Acts of the Scottish Parliament	67	6	5	1	79
Bills withdrawn	0	1	0	0	1
Bills fallen	0	6	0	0	6
Total	**67**	**13**	**5**	**1**	**86**

Note: Government bills were formerly known as executive bills

UK Supreme Court by the Advocate General for Scotland, the lord advocate or the attorney general on the grounds of legislative competence. The Secretary of State may also block legislation under section 35 of the Scotland Act 1998 (on various grounds, including defence and national security). The bill may, however, be submitted for royal assent after less than four weeks if all three Law Officers and the Secretary of State notify the Presiding Officer that they do not intend to exercise their powers under those sections.

> The monarch must give their consent for a bill to become a law; this is called royal assent. It is a final check in a constitutional monarchy that parliament is doing a proper job in passing laws that will be suitable for the country.

The passage of legislation and minority governance

For the second time in Scottish parliamentary history, the SNP govern Scotland as a minority government. This means the SNP have to compromise with other parties so they do not block legislation at every turn. This outcome empowers the Scottish Parliament, making it more like an actual legislature where compromise is at the heart of policy making. Minority government also ensures a more consensual approach to policy making, where different views and ideas are shared and more voices are heard. For example, with six MSPs the Scottish Greens hope to promote environmental and ecological issues during relevant policy formation. Research shows that ideology, policy preferences, electoral incentives and even personality factors can influence the behaviour of politicians. In an ideological sense, the SNP is fortunate to have parties both to its left and to its right, making it easier to get bills passed. As the SNP have 63 out of 129 seats, they only require the support of two MSPs, presuming their own MSPs vote accordingly.

The stages and passage of a bill

Bills need to complete three stages to become an Act of the Scottish Parliament. Committees are heavily involved from the beginning of the legislative process through to scrutinising proposed legislation.

Stage 1: general principles (committee)

The bill is referred to the committee with the relevant subject remit, known as the lead committee. Other committees can also consider and report their views to the lead committee. In addition, the lead committee must take account of any views submitted to it by the Finance Committee. The lead committee will make recommendations about whether parliament should agree to the bill's general principles.

Stage 2: detailed consideration (committee)

If parliament agrees to the general principles of the bill at stage 1, it then proceeds to stage 2. Here it will receive more detailed, line-by-line scrutiny by the lead committee. The committee will also consider any proposed amendments put forward by MSPs and will decide which amendments to accept. At this stage, the committee can also take further evidence.

Stage 3: further detailed consideration (parliament)

If the bill proceeds to stage 3, the whole parliament will then consider and vote on whether to pass it in its amended and final form. If parliament passes the bill it goes forward for royal assent, becoming an Act of the Scottish Parliament.

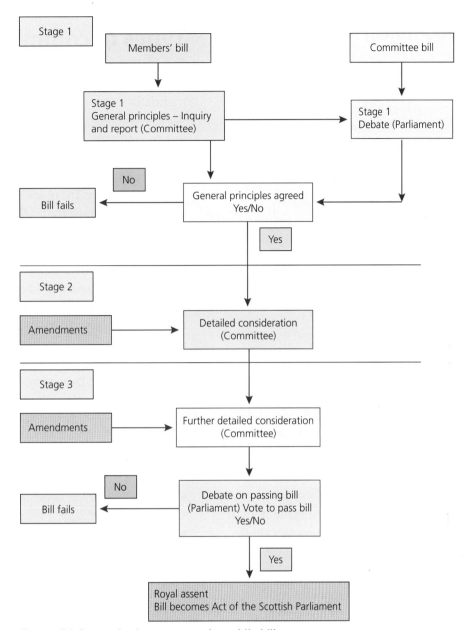

Figure 5.2 **Stages in the passage of a public bill**

Show your understanding

1 What is pre-legislative consultation?
2 Create a spider diagram showing the various types of bills that can be introduced in the Scottish Parliament.
3 What role does the UK Supreme Court play with regards to Scottish Parliamentary legislation?
4 Outline the implications of minority government for passing legislation.
5 Explain the three stages of the passing of a bill.
6 What is royal assent?

Committees

Committees are small groups of MSPs who meet on a regular basis, usually on a Tuesday, Wednesday or Thursday morning, to scrutinise the work of the Scottish Government, conduct inquiries into subjects within their remit and examine legislation. The committees play an important democratic role in the Scottish Parliament because, unlike the UK Parliament at Westminster, the Scottish Parliament is a single-chamber parliament, with no upper house or second chamber. The Scottish Parliament's committee system allows for accessibility, openness and participation and it is generally accepted that the real work of the parliament is done in committee rooms. However, what makes the committee system at Holyrood even more open and accessible is the fact that it allows for the participation of as many people as possible in the democratic process. Committees often meet in public and can do so anywhere in Scotland, not just inside parliament. In fact, most committees allow the general public to attend and most committee meetings are streamed live on the Scottish Parliament website. Clearly, this is true democracy in action and certainly ensures transparency.

Types of committee

The parliament has different kinds of committee. Under parliamentary rules, it must establish mandatory committees. There are currently seven mandatory committees, including the Public Petitions Committee and the Equal Opportunities Committee. It can also set up subject committees to look at specific subjects or areas of policy. There are currently eight subject committees that reflect the Cabinet secretary portfolios. These include the Economy, Jobs and Fair Work Committee, the Education and Skills Committee and the Health and Sport Committee. However, the parliament can also establish temporary committees on a short-term basis to consider particular issues. These include private bill committees, which are established to consider a particular bill that has been introduced by a person or body who is not an MSP.

Mandatory committees

- Delegated Powers and Law Reform Committee
- Equal Opportunities Committee
- European and External Relations Committee
- Finance Committee
- Public Audit Committee
- Public Petitions Committee
- Standards, Procedures and Public Appointments Committee

Subject committees

- Economy, Jobs and Fair Work Committee
- Education and Skills Committee
- Environment, Climate Change and Land Reform Committee
- Health and Sport Committee
- Justice Committee
- Local Government and Communities Committee
- Rural Economy and Connectivity Committee
- Social Security Committee

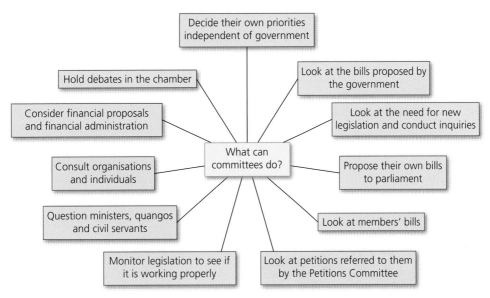

Figure 5.3 **What can committees do?**

Committee membership

The Scottish Parliament is a relatively small parliament of 129 MSPs and committee membership is restricted to MSPs who are not in the government. Most committees have between seven and eleven members, depending on the role and remit of the committee. The appointment of members takes account of the balance of the various political parties and groupings in the parliament, with all MSPs normally being on at least one committee but occasionally two. The Parliamentary Bureau (see box) can also recommend changes to the membership or make-up of committees. As committees comprise various political party members this should, in theory, ensure rigorous debate, scrutiny and accountability.

> The Parliamentary Bureau is a group of MSPs representing political parties and groupings with five or more MSPs in the parliament. They meet regularly to discuss the parliament's business and propose its business programme.

All committees are chaired by a convener and meet regularly – either weekly or fortnightly, depending on their workload. The members of the committee choose a convener from a political party following a recommendation by the Parliamentary Bureau (based on party numbers in parliament). In addition, each committee normally has a deputy convener who will chair meetings in the convener's absence. Deputy conveners are chosen in the same way as conveners. These are important roles because conveners can set the committee agenda, steering what is discussed and – sometimes more importantly – what is not discussed. Ordinary committee members can raise issues during meetings and get their concerns recorded. They can also attend and speak at any committee meetings, including those they are not a member of, but they can only vote in their own committees. Because of the strength of party discipline, committee members usually follow their party line, but there is sometimes a conflict of interest between their constituents' views, their party line and their own personal interests (see page 63). As the SNP hold 63 seats in parliament they therefore dominate committee membership. However, as they do not hold a majority of seats they therefore do not hold a majority on each committee like they did in 2011–16. The SNP still convene eight out of fifteen committees, but committees will be able to scrutinise the government much more effectively than last session.

The work of committees

Figure 5.4 **A Scottish Parliamentary Committee meeting**

Committees have two key functions – to scrutinise the work of the Scottish Government and to examine legislation. The majority of committees' work is carried out when they have to:

- scrutinise the activities of the Scottish Government
- scrutinise a proposal or draft bill
- investigate a matter
- decide whether to propose a committee bill
- consider a bill
- consider proposals for members' bills
- consider and report on subordinate legislation.

Their work involves the following three main areas:

Legislation

Every piece of legislation coming out of Holyrood will have come under the scrutiny of one or more of the Scottish Parliament's committees; therefore, it is through the function of committees that the Scottish Government is held

to account by the parliament. Out of the three stages in the passage of a bill, the legislation is scrutinised by a committee at two of them (stages 1 and 2) before the whole parliament debates and votes whether to pass it at stage 3 (see Figure 5.2).

> Subordinate legislation – an Act (primary legislation) may delegate power to a government minister to make orders, regulations or rules relating to the Act. This is known as subordinate (or secondary) legislation. Often, the details of an Act, for example, those concerning timing, implementation or the mechanism for updating, are left to subordinate legislation.

Inquiries

Committees can investigate any area that is within their remit and affects the people of Scotland, and can publish a report setting out their recommendations. Past inquiry reports have included food bank funding and eating disorders. These reports are normally discussed at a meeting of the full parliament, and as a consequence have influenced government policies and resulted in changes to legislation. Inquiries can also be conducted into how legislation passed by the parliament has worked in practice – this is sometimes referred to as 'post-legislative scrutiny'. In some cases, committees will wish to bring areas of Scottish Government policy under detailed scrutiny and hold ministers to account. In 2016 the Infrastructure and Capital Investment Committee held an inquiry into the circumstances surrounding the closure of the Forth Road Bridge in late 2015. Specifically, the remit of the inquiry was: 'To examine the management, monitoring and maintenance of the Forth Road Bridge principally in the 10-year period prior to its closure on public safety grounds in December 2015.' This inquiry put the SNP administration under intense scrutiny as the Government made budget cuts and cancelled maintenance in the years preceding the closure.

Other areas

Committees can also consider and report on government policy and actions, on European legislation, on secondary (or subordinate) legislation and on public petitions concerning the people of Scotland.

Public Petitions Committee

The Public Petitions Committee (PPC) is the main way for members of the public to influence government policy in Holyrood. The PPC will consider petitions and make a decision on the course of action to be taken in each case. The PPC has several courses of action it may take. It decides whether the parliament as a whole should debate the issue, whether a specific committee should deal with it or whether it is more appropriate for another body to consider the petition. All committees have a responsibility to consider and report on petitions sent to them. Petitions are submitted by individuals and groups who want to raise an issue and many petitions are driven by the experience of petitioners at a local level, for example, a campaign to stop a local school closure or prevent development on a local playing field. While the PPC cannot become directly involved in such matters it can ask the Scottish Government to review the wider national policies and/or guidance which govern the actions of local authorities and other public bodies. The public petitions system is a key part of the Scottish Parliament's commitment to openness and accessibility. Petitions can have positive outcomes that lead to change or inform debate – the smoking ban was first raised as a public petition.

Case study: Committee achievements in challenging government and influencing policy (parliamentary session 4, 2011–16)

- The Justice Sub-Committee on Policing questioned Police Scotland on matters such as response times and stop and search – a policy change on stop and search was announced during a committee questioning session.
- The Public Petitions Committee has achieved several changes to policy through highlighting matters raised in petitions. For example, in response to a petition on chronic pain, the Government announced the establishment of a chronic pain centre.
- The Justice Committee's report on the Human Trafficking and Exploitation Bill suggested a number of improvements which led to Scottish Government amendments.
- The European and External Relations Committee responded to rising concerns about the Transatlantic Trade and Investment Partnership (TTIP) by holding an urgent inquiry, with evidence from trade unions, the third sector and business. This was followed by an evening event hosted with the European Parliament where the public could raise concerns about TTIP.
- The Education and Culture Committee's Stage 1 report on the Education (Scotland) Bill, particularly the section on additional support for learning, prompted the Scottish Government to make a series of amendments to the Bill.

Case study: Does the Scottish Parliament scrutinise legislation effectively enough?

The Scottish Parliament was designed to be a powerful and effective Legislature with committees at the heart of its work. This aim was outlined in the final report of the Scottish Constitutional Convention, which expected a 'parliament to operate through a system of powerful committees which are able to initiate legislation as well as to scrutinise and amend government proposals, and which have wide-ranging investigative functions'. The parliament has combined standing and select committee functions to help develop expertise within the committees responsible for scrutinising legislation. Most committees are permanent and not subject to government dissolution. They have relatively few members to allow them to develop a 'businesslike', not partisan, culture. The number of convenors (chairs) is proportional by party and they are selected by each committee. Committee deliberation takes place before the initial and final plenary stages. Committees can invite witnesses and demand government documents and they have an unusual role which involves the monitoring of the Scottish Government's pre-legislative consultation. Further, if all else fails, they have the ability to initiate their own bills (as can individual MSPs) in a much more straightforward way than in Westminster.

However, the Scottish Parliament was not designed to be a powerful Legislature in the way that we associate with political systems such as the United States. Crucially, there are not the same divisions of powers and checks and balances between Executive, Legislature and Judiciary. Instead, the Executive operates at the heart of the Legislature and, when enjoying a single or coalition party majority, has the ability to control its procedures. Furthermore, committees are said to be hamstrung by the amount of legislation they have to scrutinise with most bills being fairly innocuous and receiving cross-party support. This stops committees rarely setting the agenda for future Scottish Government action by, for example, identifying gaps in existing policy and prompting further action by introducing committee bills. In relation, when it comes to conducting inquiries, many inquiries have been charged with partisanship and do not produce meaningful advice and engagement with government. As mentioned earlier, the SNP dominates committee membership and convenership, and MSPs toe the party line. Lastly, effective scrutiny requires the Scottish Parliament to have a sufficient number of staff able to devote their time and attention to the policy work and legislation of the Scottish Government. However, the Scottish Parliament employs relatively few relevant staff compared to Westminster.

Source: *Adapted from a paper by Paul Cairney of Stirling University, January 2016*

ICT task

Visit the Scottish Parliament website and research the current petitions being considered by the Public Petitions Committee.

Added Value idea

The scrutinising powers of the Scottish Parliament have come under criticism for being inadequate. You could research options such as increasing the size of parliament or introducing a second chamber.

Show your understanding

1 Why are committees important to the democratic functioning of the Scottish Parliament?
2 Describe the two types of committee.
3 Describe the membership setup of committees.
4 Why is the role of convener important?
5 Describe the main areas of work done by committees.
6 Explain the role and remit of the Public Petitions Committee.
7 Read the case study on the effectiveness of parliament scrutiny. Create a table with arguments for and against the Scottish Parliament's effectiveness at scrutinising the government.

12-mark questions

1 Evaluate the effectiveness of parliamentary representatives in holding the government to account.
2 Evaluate the effectiveness of committees in holding the government to account.

20-mark question

To what extent is the Scottish Parliament successful in holding the government to account?

The Scottish Executive

The Scottish Government (legally referred to as The Scottish Executive) is the government in Scotland in charge of devolved matters. The Scottish Executive is responsible for formulating and implementing policy in these areas and is led by the first minister, who is nominated by the parliament and appointed by the monarch. He or she in turn appoints Scottish ministers to make up a Cabinet, but only with the agreement of parliament and the approval of the monarch. Cabinet members are referred to as Cabinet secretaries.

The role of the first minister and the Executive

The first minister is the head of the devolved Scottish Government. He or she leads the Scottish Cabinet and is responsible for the development, implementation and presentation of government policy, constitutional affairs and promoting and representing Scotland. The first minister is also directly accountable to the Scottish Parliament for his or her actions and the actions of the Scottish Government. There is no fixed term of office for the first minister and, after appointment, the first minister can remain in position until he or she resigns, is dismissed or dies.

There have only been five first ministers in the short history of the Scottish Parliament: the first, Donald Dewar, died in office and the second, Henry McLeish, resigned. In both of these circumstances, it was the responsibility of the presiding officer to appoint someone to serve as first minister in the interim, until the Scottish Parliament decided on a new nominee to be presented to the monarch for formal appointment. The third, Jack McConnell, left office after the 2007 election saw the SNP become the biggest party in the parliament with Alex Salmond named as first minister. When Alex Salmond resigned after the 2014 referendum result, Nicola Sturgeon became first minister. Sturgeon remains in post following the SNP's victory in 2016.

The role of the first minister

The first minister has the power to appoint MSPs to become Cabinet secretaries and ministers who form the Executive. She also has the power to 'reshuffle' the Cabinet and replace any secretaries whom she feels are underperforming. The first minister sets the agenda and chairs Cabinet meetings and is primarily responsible for the formulation and introduction of Scottish Government policy. The first minister is also the face of the Scottish Government and represents Scotland in devolved matters as well as representing Scotland abroad when building foreign relations. The first minister's powers are kept in check by being held accountable to the Scottish Parliament. The first minister faces questions every Thursday in First Minister's Question Time, where opposition leaders scrutinise the government's work. Nicola Sturgeon may also appear in front of committees to face scrutiny.

Figure 5.5 First Minister's Question Time

The term 'Scottish ministers' collectively refers to the first minister, the Cabinet secretaries, the lord advocate and the solicitor general, who together make up the Scottish Government. Each Cabinet secretary is responsible for a particular department and will indicate to the parliament what actions his or her department intends to take, and what legislation it wants the parliament to agree to. The government is accountable to the parliament for its actions. In the 2011–16 Scottish Parliament, the SNP held a majority of seats: 69 out of 129. This allowed the SNP to push on with implementing their policies as they could rely on majority support in parliament. However, since the 2016 elections, the SNP no longer holds a majority of seats. This means that the SNP Government will have to work with other parties to pass legislation. The SNP's 2014 referendum was only achievable due to their 2011 majority. Furthermore, the lord advocate (the chief legal officer of the Scottish Government) and the solicitor general are members of the Scottish Executive, as set out in the Scotland Act (1998). However, after becoming first minister Alex Salmond decided that the lord advocate should no longer attend the Scottish Cabinet, stating that he wished to 'de-politicise the post'.

The Scottish Government is responsible for devolved matters, most of which affect the day-to-day lives of the people of Scotland, for example, health, education, justice, rural affairs and transport. It manages an annual budget of around £35 billion and each Cabinet secretary is responsible for a particular department. Ministers are therefore part of two separate organisations: the Scottish Executive (as Cabinet secretaries or ministers) and the Scottish Parliament (as MSPs). In addition to a constituency or regional office dealing with local matters, they may also have a ministerial office within a Scottish Executive building dealing with ministerial responsibilities. The term 'Scottish Government' is also used as a collective term to describe Scottish ministers, including civil servants. The Scottish Government and the Scottish Parliament are accountable to the people of Scotland.

The Scottish Cabinet

Figure 5.6 **The 2016 Scottish Cabinet**

The Scottish Cabinet usually meets on a weekly basis, but only while parliament is sitting. It consists of the first minister and other Scottish ministers (Cabinet secretaries), excluding the Scottish law officers (the lord advocate and the solicitor general). The lord advocate attends meetings of the Cabinet only when requested by the first minister.

The Scottish Government operates on the basis of collective responsibility. This means that all decisions reached by ministers, individually or collectively, are binding on all members of the government. Collective responsibility does not mean that ministers must all agree on decisions; instead, membership of the government requires them to maintain a united front once decisions have been made. The 2016–21 Scottish Government consists of ten Cabinet secretaries (including the first minister), twelve ministers and two law officers.

The civil service

The civil service in Scotland is part of the wider UK home civil service as it is a matter reserved by the UK Parliament and not a matter devolved to the Scottish Parliament. While the permanent secretary of the Scottish civil service, Leslie Evans, is the most senior civil servant in Scotland and heads the strategic board of the Scottish Executive, she remains answerable to the most senior civil servant in the UK, the Cabinet secretary. However, those civil servants who work for the Scottish Government primarily serve the devolved administration rather than the UK Government.

Potential conflict

The Civil Service Code (Scottish Executive version) states that civil servants in Scotland are 'accountable to Scottish ministers who are, in turn, accountable to the Scottish Parliament'; and it advises that they are at the same time 'an integral and key part of the government of the United Kingdom'. This is a compromising situation and some argue that civil servants working for the Scottish Government owe their loyalty to the devolved administration rather than to the UK Government. Currently, civil servants in Scotland are working directly for an SNP administration and their colleagues in London are working directly for a Conservative administration. This sounds problematic but the civil service has to remain politically neutral and unbiased on issues such as independence.

Nevertheless, the core problem is that in reality the civil service is serving two governments of different political ideologies at the same time. Therefore, a situation of conflict could develop when a civil servant serving a Conservative minister in Westminster has to talk to or brief a civil servant in Edinburgh who serves an SNP minister. If the matter is a confidential one, the exchange of details may be restrained and limited because they both know that the information will be shared with the opposing ministers.

The Sewel Convention

A Legislative Consent Motion (formerly a Sewel Motion) is when, in certain circumstances, the Scottish Parliament may give its consent for Westminster to legislate for Scotland on devolved matters. Some government policies on reserved matters can have significant implications for Scotland through their potential impact on the policies of the Scottish Government, which will have to implement them in Scotland. Generally speaking, however, Legislative Consent Motions work in favour of the Scottish Parliament as they are only used when it would be more effective to legislate on a UK basis in order to put in place a single UK-wide ruling (for example, powers for the courts to confiscate the assets of serious offenders). Furthermore, a Legislative Consent Motion ensures that Westminster will normally legislate on devolved matters only with the express agreement of the Scottish Parliament, after proper consideration and scrutiny of the proposal in question. To facilitate that scrutiny, the UK Government advises the Scottish Parliament as early as possible of any bill that is likely to be subject to a Legislative Consent Motion and will provide the relevant committee with a detailed memorandum explaining the purpose and effect of any devolved provisions as soon as possible after it is introduced. The committee will then be able to consider the proposal, taking evidence from interested parties if it considers that necessary, before making a recommendation to the full parliament as to

whether it should approve the Legislative Consent Motion. The Scottish Parliament is free to withhold consent and reject a motion. However, it could be argued that this set-up highlights that Westminster is still the more powerful partner in the arrangement.

Financing the Scottish Government

One of the most controversial questions facing politicians on both sides of the border is how the Scottish Government is financed. Differences of opinion over it can threaten good relations between Scotland and the rest of the UK. It is not a new question insofar as it has long been claimed that Scotland received more than its fair share of British public expenditure in the pre-devolution era. Such 'discrepancies' are partly based on different levels of deprivation across British regions. In respect of Scotland's apparently favoured and privileged position, part of the explanation lies in its relatively large territorial size and low population density outside the central belt, which means that expenditure per person for the same level of services such as education and health care is higher (Scotland's population is roughly 10 per cent of England's). With an SNP administration in Holyrood and a Conservative Government in Westminster, there is an intensification of the controversy along national lines, with English regions renewing their complaint that they are unfairly treated and the Scots replying that the differentials are justifiable on the grounds of need and Scotland's contribution to the British Treasury from North Sea oil revenues. The ultimate catch-22 situation for any English politicians looking for a reduction in Scottish public expenditure is that cutting Scotland's budget might strengthen the SNP's case for independence referendum number two (see page 26 for the new fiscal framework).

The Barnett formula

Essentially the formula means that for every £1 the UK Government distributes, 85p goes to England, 10p to Scotland and 5p to Wales. With a population of five million people, Scotland has only around 8 per cent of the UK population but gets a fixed quota of 10 per cent of the cash for public services. That has led to a situation where spending in Scotland on public services is £1,500 higher per person than in England.

English politicians and newspapers have criticised the formula as being unfair to England. On the BBC's *Question Time*, a *Daily Mail* columnist, Kelvin MacKenzie, declared that the Scots were ripping off the English. He stated that 'basically the Scots exist solely on the handouts of the clever English generating wealth in London and the south-east'. This viewpoint has been challenged in Scotland.

Relations with Westminster

Since 2011 and the SNP's rise to a position of considerable power, relations between the Scottish Government and Westminster have been strained. In the course of that period was the 2014 independence referendum which almost put an end to the UK as we know it. Currently, the SNP holds power, enjoys huge support in Scotland and still has independence as their principle aim. The UK has a Conservative Government, which remains incredibly unpopular in Scotland, as well as being further to the right politically than the SNP. Added to this, the result of the 2015 UK General Election sent 56 SNP MPs to Westminster who continue to oppose Conservative policy on a daily basis. The 2015 UK election only served to highlight again the limited influence Scots have on UK politics with Scotland returning only one Conservative MP. You should also read pages 23–25 on English votes for English laws.

Conflict with Westminster

Brexit

The result of the June 2016 EU Referendum created further constitutional tension between Scotland and the rest of the UK. A majority (62%) of the Scottish population voted for the UK to remain in the European Union but, overall, 52% of the UK population voted for the UK to leave the EU. After the result, Nicola Sturgeon stated it would be 'democratically unacceptable' for Scotland to be taken out of the European Union against the wishes of its people.

The Alistair Carmichael memo scandal

Relations between the Scottish Government and the UK Government were particularly strained in the lead-up to the 2015 UK General Election when former Secretary of State for Scotland, Alistair Carmichael, released a memo slandering Nicola Sturgeon. Carmichael authorised his special adviser to release a memo to the *Telegraph* newspaper about a private conversation in which Scotland's First Minister purportedly said she wanted David Cameron to remain as prime minister. Nicola Sturgeon claimed the memo was '100 per cent false' but the memo was potentially hugely damaging to the SNP leader because it suggested she was misleading voters about her preferred election outcome. Carmichael later admitted the memo was fabricated which resulted in him almost losing his job as an MP, and his reputation as a politician also suffered.

Release of the Lockerbie bomber

One of the most controversial decisions made by the Scottish Government was the 2009 release of convicted terrorist Abdelbaset Ali al-Megrahi. Prime Minister Cameron declared publicly that the decision to allow the Lockerbie bomber to return to Libya on health grounds 'undermined' the UK's global standing. Firstly, at the Tory Party conference he attacked the Scottish

Government's release of al-Megrahi. He said the decision was 'wrong' and that 'nothing like that must ever happen again'.

Then, on a visit to the USA, he said the decision to free al-Megrahi had been 'profoundly misguided' and sought to distance himself from the Scottish Government's decision. During a radio interview, he said, 'I agree that the decision to release al-Megrahi was wrong. I said it was wrong at the time. It was the Scottish Government that took that decision. I just happen to think it was profoundly misguided. He was convicted of the biggest mass murder and in my view he should have died in jail. I said that very, very clearly at the time; that is my view today. But let's be clear about who released al-Megrahi … it was the decision of Scottish ministers.'

The Bedroom Tax

The Bedroom Tax was introduced by the Conservative–Liberal Democrat Coalition Government in 2013 and has been one of the most controversial policies in recent years. Its aim is to encourage those living in larger council houses to downsize and so reduce waiting times for larger families in finding suitable accommodation. In encouraging people to downsize, the UK Government penalises under-occupancy by cutting housing benefit if residents live in a council or housing association property and have what is classified as a 'spare' bedroom.

However, the SNP-led Scottish Government is highly critical and fiercely opposed to the Bedroom Tax. The Scottish Government invested a total of £90 million between 2013 and 2016 in discretionary housing payments to fully mitigate the impact of the Bedroom Tax for affected Scottish households. The Scottish Government argued 'the money was millions of pounds of investment which should not have been diverted away from other areas since we would not introduce and do not support the UK Government's policy'.

The international refugee crisis

More than a million refugees crossed into Europe in 2015 and 2016, sparking a crisis as countries struggled to cope with the influx. The UK Government's response was controversial as it opted out of an EU plan to settle refugees around Europe. Former Prime Minister David Cameron instead stated that the UK would accept up to 20,000 refugees from Syria over the next five years. However, this pales in comparison to Germany where around 800,000 refugees were settled in 2015.

The Scottish Government was at odds with the decision of the UK Government towards accepting refugees. Nicola Sturgeon stated, 'the people of the UK will be haunted for generations if they did not help those in need … the UK needs to take its fair and proportionate share of those seeking help'.

Trident

The UK Government has voted to renew Trident, the country's nuclear submarine system, while the Scottish Parliament voted against renewing it. However, the issue of renewing Britain's nuclear deterrent is reserved by Westminster and as far as the UK Government is concerned the decision has been made.

The Secretary of State for Scotland

Figure 5.7 **David Mundell MP, Secretary of State for Scotland**

The Secretary of State for Scotland is a UK minister who represents the interests of Scotland in the UK Government, particularly those matters reserved to the UK Government. He or she heads up the Scotland Office, which is the government department responsible for Scottish affairs at Westminster. In late 2015, the Scotland Office re-branded their Facebook profile to 'UK Government for Scotland' and at the same time changed the Scotland Office Twitter handle to @UKGovScotland. This was in response to concerns that many Scottish people were unsure of the role of the Scotland Office and to emphasise that Scotland had two governments.

David Mundell, Scotland's only Scottish Conservative MP, is the present Secretary for State for Scotland. He is responsible for the smooth running of Scotland's devolution settlement and is the UK minister responsible for the passing of the Scotland Act. Critics have called him Scotland's Governor General as they argue that the Scottish people overwhelmingly rejected the Conservatives in the May 2015 General Election. Many Scots regard him as being the apologist and defender of unpopular policies imposed by the Conservative Government.

Despite widespread support from Scottish business and university principals for Scotland to be allowed to introduce its own visa scheme for international graduates, David Mundell refused to devolve this power as part of the Scotland Act. Scotland's population is ageing and is relatively declining compared to England, so an influx of young, highly skilled professionals meets Scotland's needs. In contrast England is experiencing a rapid increase in its immigrant population and the Conservative Government has promised to reduce their numbers.

All political parties in Scotland including the Scottish Conservatives support an independent visa scheme for Scotland, yet David Mundell must support what suits England. Universities in

> ## Show your understanding
>
> 1 Outline the various positions that make up the Scottish Government.
> 2 Describe the role of the first minister.
> 3 What is meant by collective responsibility?
> 4 a) What is the role of the civil service?
>   b) Why might there be conflict within the civil service?
> 5 Explain the Sewel Convention.
> 6 Describe in detail how the Scottish Government is financed. Refer to the Barnett formula.
> 7 Since the SNP's rise to power, why have relations between the Scottish Government and Westminster worsened?
> 8 Describe two areas of conflict between the Scottish Government and Westminster.
> 9 Outline the role of the Secretary State for Scotland.
>
> ## 12-mark question
>
> Analyse the relationship between the Scottish Government and the UK Government.

Scotland argue that the new scheme imposed has cost the Scottish economy £250 million. Under the new scheme an international student is given just four months to find a graduate level job paying at least £20,500 or they will be forced to leave Scotland and the UK.

Relations with local government

In Scotland there are 32 local authorities (often referred to as councils). Some of these councils are based on county borders and cover a large geographical area while others are based on city boundaries, for example, Edinburgh and Glasgow. These local councils have a key role in communities and impact on the daily lives of all Scottish citizens. They provide vital public services, including schools for the children and care for the elderly; they also maintain the roads, collect the refuse and provide facilities for leisure and recreation. The range of services provided by these councils is extensive and the money to pay for them comes from a combination of council tax and grants from the Scottish Government, which in turn gets its money from the UK Government. Councils spend around £20 billion each year, employ around 250,000 staff and use assets worth about £32 billion.

COSLA

The Convention of Scottish Local Authorities (COSLA) is the national representative body and voice for local government in Scotland. COSLA works to promote the position of local government and has to regularly communicate the position of the 32 local authorities to the Scottish Government.

Conflict with local government

As the Scottish Parliament sets the agenda for most of the functions carried out by local authorities, the Scottish Government sets the parameters of government policy for local government to put into practice, and also sets targets for local government to achieve. For their relationship to work effectively there must be clear co-operation and communication. The Scottish Government needs local councils to implement government policy. Likewise, local authorities need the Scottish Government to give advice and assistance on their functions because of the legal constraints within which they must operate. More importantly, local government is reliant on the Scottish Government for income through the revenue support grant. However, this interdependent functioning doesn't always run smoothly and there is always the issue of party politics as well. With the SNP in power nationally, there is obviously going to be conflict with local governments that are under the control of rival political parties or coalitions – and the vast majority of Scotland's local authorities are

The 2007 Concordat Agreement

The Scottish Government's concordat agreement with local government in 2007 changed the relationship between the two parties and led to a sizeable shift in decision making from national to local government. Today this relationship is based on mutual respect, partnership and progress. Furthermore, the development of single outcome agreements (SOAs), which give local authorities greater freedom to set their own priorities, is an important part of these changes. SOAs set out the outcomes which each local authority is seeking to achieve and reflect local needs, circumstances and priorities, but are also related to the relevant national outcomes set by the Scottish Government.

The intention was to ensure the alignment of funding and activities within local authorities and other areas of the public sector with the Scottish Government's priorities and national outcomes. To achieve this aim, the following four key tenets are included in the concordat:

- Collaborative working and joint accountability: the relationship between central and local government is based on mutual respect and partnership, and enables local authorities to respond more effectively to local needs.
- Finance and funding: financial decisions are taken locally and ring-fencing is reduced.
- Reduced bureaucracy: less micro-management by central government.
- SOAs: align local policy with overall government targets, taking account of local priorities.

coalition run. This provides the potential for conflict between two democratic legitimacies: on the one hand, the democratic legitimacy of Scotland's 32 local authorities; on the other, the democratic legitimacy of both the Scottish Parliament and the Scottish Government. For example, one of the SNP's key priorities is to maintain the number of teachers working in Scotland. As teachers are employed by local authorities, the government has to work closely with authorities to ensure this priority is a success. However, some local authorities, in aiming to meet budget demands, have cut teacher numbers.

Funding

Local government receives most of its income (around 80 per cent) directly from the Scottish Government in the form of grants. The remaining 20 per cent is raised locally by the council itself from council tax payments and various fees and charges for the services they provide. From 2007, the Scottish Government has provided additional funding to allow local authorities to freeze their council tax levels (see case study below). It is the responsibility of each local authority to allocate the total financial resources available to it (excluding ring-fenced resources) on the basis of local needs and priorities, whilst including the Scottish Government's key objectives.

Negotiations take place between Scottish ministers and COSLA as part of the spending review process, which takes place every two or three years. In order to ensure a fair and equitable distribution of finance between councils, some local authorities receive more money from the Scottish Government than others. This is because not all local authorities are the same size and therefore do not have the same revenue-raising potential. For example, the largest local authority is Glasgow City Council, which has a population of around 600,000; the smallest local authority is Orkney, with a population of fewer than 20,000. Also, Glasgow is home to seventeen of the twenty poorest areas in Scotland, with the top ten most deprived council wards in Scotland all being in the city. Just over half of Glasgow's population lives in these most deprived areas. The four authorities with the next biggest proportions of deprivation are Inverclyde (39.1 per cent), Dundee (30.7 per cent), West Dunbartonshire (26.3 per cent) and North Ayrshire (25 per cent).

Case study: Strained relations – council tax freeze and changes

A flagship policy of the SNP since 2007 has been to freeze council tax. This policy was highly controversial because local councils struggled to balance budgets as a consequence of the economic turmoil of the last decade. As an incentive not to increase council tax, councils were given extra money each year to cover the costs of freezing the tax and extra funding specifically to target sectors such as social care. If a council put the tax up, it lost this extra cash and faced a penalty charge. Councils felt like their hands were tied and the council tax freeze was a constant bone of contention between national and local government.

In 2016 the SNP reformed council tax, which saw an increase in tax for those living in more expensive houses. Council tax is based on the value of property and is set against a band system that goes from A–H, H being the highest value. The SNP increased the rate of council tax for those living in bands E–H. Those living in band E homes will pay an extra £105 per year with those in band H paying £517 extra. Furthermore, local authorities will be allowed to increase council tax by 3 per cent at their own discretion to raise extra funds.

Show your understanding

1 Describe the system of local government in Scotland.
2 Outline the ways that the 2007 Concordat Agreement hopes to promote positive relations between national and local government.
3 Explain the various reasons why the Scottish Government has conflict with local government.
4 Explain why some councils receive more money from the Scottish Government than others.

6 Representative democracy in the United Kingdom

As mentioned in Chapter 1, the UK's political system is a parliamentary democracy with a constitutional monarchy in which the country is managed by a process involving elected representatives and various institutions. These institutions work together in maintaining, developing and creating new laws that drive forward change. Judgement of the success and/or failures of these changes takes place every five years when most of the UK's citizens vote in a general election. Following this election, it is often the case that new representatives are elected as Members of Parliament (MPs) and a new government is formed to drive forward further change.

The role of political representatives

Each MP represents all of the people within their constituency regardless of whether they voted for them or not. Additionally, MPs are usually also members of a political party and so are expected to support their party leader and the party's policies. This can cause conflict at times, especially if policies have negative effects on their constituents. However, voters vote not only for the individual but also because of their affiliation with a party and so MPs are expected by constituents to support the aims of the party as well.

The majority of MPs are known as 'backbenchers'. This means that they have not been promoted to the government or shadow government. These backbenchers have many opportunities to influence the decision-making process. When in parliament, MPs will be busy carrying out some of the following roles:

- Asking government ministers questions on behalf of their constituents or other interested organisations. On most occasions this will take the form of written questions, and government ministers must respond to these. This can be at any Ministers Questions sessions, or by sending internal email/letters to a government department.
- Debating on key issues affecting the country and on legislation that may be passing through parliament. This can take the form of a debate in the Westminster Hall or Adjournment Debates of the Commons chamber.
- As members of committees they will also have a number of duties to carry out including meetings, interviewing key stakeholders and other correspondence.
- Creating their own Early Day Motions which highlight issues that may lead on to a debate in the chamber. Also on occasion creating a Private Members Bill which if selected by ballot can become an Act of Parliament.
- Lastly, and most crucially, they vote on legislation. All MPs have one vote each and so during divisons all MPs, in theory, have equal power.

Representation

A key issue with parliament is whether it accurately represents the population of the UK. One criticism is the social class and educational background of MPs. After the general election in

2015 it was found that 32 per cent of MPs went to a fee-paying school, even though these schools educate just 7 per cent of the population. Also, one in ten of these privately educated MPs went to the same secondary school – Eton. David Cameron was the nineteenth prime minister to have been educated at Eton. Of the 427 winning candidates who went to university, 131 (31 per cent) went to either Oxford or Cambridge University. After the last election it was noted that 34 per cent of all Tory MPs and 17 per cent of Labour MPs had been to Oxbridge. According to the Sutton Trust's chief executive Dr Lee Elliot Major, 'If Parliament is truly to represent the whole nation, the best people should be able to become MPs, regardless of social background.'

In addition to social background the number of female MPs is also an issue for the House of Commons. Traditionally, women have been greatly under-represented in Westminster. In 1979 only 19 MPs were women. However, since then the situation has significantly improved (see Table 6.1) The number of female MPs rose from 147 (22 per cent) in 2010 to 191 (29 per cent) in 2015. The Conservatives and Labour both witnessed a jump in the number of female MPs and the SNP also brought 20 female MPs into the mix. However, the House of Commons compares poorly in this respect to Sweden (45 per cent), Belgium (41.3 per cent) and Argentina (36 per cent).

The 2015 General Election also witnessed improvements for the representation of BMEs in Westminster. BME MPs made up more than 6 per cent of the 2015 parliament, up from 4.2 per cent in 2010 – a 30 per cent increase. Now 42 minority-ethnic MPs sit in the Commons, building on the success of the 2010 election, when 27 BME MPs won seats in Westminster. Among them is the first MP of Chinese origin, Alan Mak, who won the Havant constituency for the Conservatives.

Lastly, the age of MPs has also been a source of criticism. The average age of MPs in 2015 was 51 years of age and this is consistent with previous parliaments. Indeed since 1979 the lowest average age has been 49 with the highest 51. This is despite the influx of younger SNP MPs in 2015 such as Mhairi Black MP for Paisley and Renfrewshire South, who became the youngest ever UK parliamentarian at only 20 years of age.

Figure 6.1 Mhairi Black MP (above) and Alan Mak MP (below)

Table 6.1 Gender and racial composition of MPs 1987–2015

	Gender		Racial composition	
	Male	Female	White	BME
1987	609	41 (6%)	646	4 (0.6%)
1992	591	60 (9%)	645	6 (0.9%)
1997	539	120 (18%)	650	9 (1.4%)
2001	541	118 (18%)	647	12 (1.8%)
2005	518	128 (20%)	631	15 (2.3%)
2010	507	143 (22%)	623	27 (4.2%)
2015	459	191 (29%)	608	42 (6.6%)

Limitations on representation

Party loyalty

At the centre of this debate is the fact that MPs must balance their role as representatives of citizens with the aims of their political party. One key aspect of the working of parliament is political parties' use of the 'whip' system. It is the job of party whips to enforce strong party discipline. The party whip ensures that MPs toe the party line and drives rebellious or straying MPs back into line with the party. Whips also act as tellers by counting votes in divisions and organising the pairing system, whereby pairs of opposing MPs both agree not to vote when either is prevented from being at Westminster.

The big dilemma for MPs arises when there is a conflict of interest. In most cases, MPs do as their party wishes and vote when and as instructed by the whips. However, in December 2015, the new Labour leader, Jeremy Corbyn was forced to allow Labour MPs to have a free vote over the UK bombing of Syria as a significant number of Labour MPs would have defied his wishes and voted for the bombing campaign.

Loyalty and toeing the party line can lead to reward and promotion, whereas disloyalty can lead to sanctions and ultimately removal from the party – this is known as 'withdrawing the whip' and while it does not result in the MP losing their job (they were after all given the job by their constituents) it can mean that in the next election they will not be the party's chosen candidate and so stand little chance of winning their seat again. This is also the case where the MP embarrasses the party by being accused of acting immorally or illegally. This was the case in September 2015 when the SNP suspended Michelle Thomson MP from the party over accusations of an illegal business deal. Ms Thomson is no longer a member of the SNP but she will likely remain the MP for Edinburgh West until the 2020 election.

The job of the whips becomes more important if the majority of the party in government is small or when a coalition is formed, because this can make it more likely that the government will lose major votes. Therefore, it is crucial that both government and opposition whips get as many of their MPs to vote as possible, and with their party.

Backbench rebellions

A key measure of how much power a government has is the number of backbench MPs who rebel against the whip and vote against their wishes. During the 2010–15 Coalition Government there was a record number of rebellious votes. This is largely down to the fact that the Government had to constantly compromise over the wishes of the Conservative Party and the Liberal Democrat Party. Policies put forward that were key Conservative policies did not necessarily have the full support of Liberal Democrat MPs and vice versa. For example, Conservative backbenchers forced David Cameron to go back on the coalition agreement to reform the House of Lords. In retaliation the Liberal Democrats refused to support the proposed electoral boundaries legislation and it was dropped.

According to website *publicwhip*.org.uk from 2010 to 2015 coalition MPs rebelled in a record 35 per cent of divisions. That easily beats the previous record of 28 per cent, held by the Blair/Brown Government from 2005 to 2010. In the 2015–16 Parliament the three issues that resulted in the biggest rebellions were assisted dying, airstrikes on Syria and the European Union referendum.

Table 6.2 **The House of Commons most rebellious MPs in 2015**

Philip Hollobone (Conservative)	19.9%
Philip Davie (Conservative)	19.6%
Christopher Chope (Conservative)	18.8%
David Nuttall (Conservative)	16.9%
Peter Bone (Conservative)	15.2%

Source: The *Independent*

Expenses

The public outcry over MPs' expenses in 2009 was seen as the most forceful expression of a deeper frustration with the political system. A number of MPs were forced to resign and some also ended up behind bars due to fraudulently claiming expenses. Many people began to feel that the House of Commons was not working on their behalf. The Constitutional Reform and Governance Act 2010 essentially gave huge powers to the Independent Parliamentary Standards Authority (IPSA) to better hold MPs to account over their expenses and other interests that they may have. MPs now are given a parliament debit card which allows much greater scrutiny of expenses. Every year the IPSA reviews all MPs' expenses and to date has forced many MPs to pay back expenses that have been judged to be inappropriate for office. For example, in 2015 IPSA found that 26 MPs had made inaccurate claims and they were advised to repay these claims or their names would be published. Some MPs have criticised this tactic as 'childish' as most of these sums were very low, such as individual phone calls, and did not require such a heavy-handed response.

Case study: 'Cash for access' controversy

Two former foreign secretaries faced accusations in 2015 of being involved in a 'cash for access' scandal by offering to use their political influence in return for payment.

Following a 'sting' operation, Jack Straw and Sir Malcolm Rifkind offered to use their positions as politicians on behalf of a fictitious Chinese company set up by Channel 4's *Dispatches* programme in return for payments of at least £5,000 per day. Straw, for many years one of Labour's most senior figures, claimed that he operated 'under the radar' to use his influence to change European Union ⇨

Case study continued...

rules on behalf of a commodity firm which paid him £60,000 a year. He also claimed to have used 'charm and menace' to convince the Ukrainian Prime Minister to change laws on behalf of the same firm.

Straw referred himself to the parliamentary commissioner for standards and suspended himself from the parliamentary Labour Party. Rifkind also referred himself to the parliamentary commissioner for standards. Both men were cleared by the commissioner as they did not breach parliamentary rules because they had disclosed their activities and financial interests at the relevant time in the register of members' interests. They both did not stand in the 2015 election and therefore are no longer MPs.

But the story raised the broader, complex debate on whether MPs or peers should be allowed to hold second jobs that allow them to lobby on legislation, or any other political issue, on behalf of private commercial interests.

Source: *Adapted from the* Guardian, *23 February 2015*

Show your understanding

1. Explain the role of party whips.
2. In what ways can a party punish MPs who defy their wishes?
3. What are backbench rebellions?
4. Why did the 2010–15 Coalition Government suffer a record number of backbench rebellions?
5. What steps has parliament taken to improve the ways in which MPs claim expenses?
6. With reference to the 'cash for access' case study, describe the main issues with 'lobbying' ministers.

The Legislature and Executive in the United Kingdom

People often confuse parliament with government and vice versa. While they work hand-in-glove with each other in the creation of laws they are completely separate institutions.

The government runs the country by driving forward its ideas and attempting to turn them into new bills and by implementing its own policies. Thus the government can also be referred to as the Executive. Parliament essentially acts as a 'checkpoint' for the government by ensuring that the work of government is scrutinsed, people are held to account, bills are thoroughly examined and finally approved into law. Parliament is the highest legislative authority in the UK and so is referred to as the Legislature. Although it is not part of the making of laws, a key element in the evaluation of government policy is the Judiciary. These are the courts that often process the government acts and controversially can challenge the Executive and Legislature on occasion.

The Legislature

The UK Parliament is made up of three parts: the House of Commons, the House of Lords and the monarch (the king or queen). All three institutions combine to carry out the work of parliament. The Legislature in the UK is bicameral. This means that legislative business takes place in two chambers or houses – the House of Commons and the House of Lords.

Legislation

The primary function of parliament is to make laws and change existing laws (legislation). However, a new law must pass through and complete a series of stages in both the House of Commons and the House of Lords, with mutual agreement by both, before it is finally approved.

A bill, which can begin in either house, is a proposal for a new law or a proposal to change an existing law and is debated in parliament. Either house can vote down a bill, in which case it will normally not become law, but there are exceptions. The Commons can pass the same bill in two successive years, in which case it can become law without the agreement of the Lords. Bills that are only about money (raising taxes or authorising government expenditure) are usually not opposed in the Lords (see page 98) and may only be delayed for a month. The monarch must approve the bill by signing it – this is known as royal assent. At this point, the bill becomes an Act of Parliament and is a law.

The process by which a bill becomes a law is characterised by a series of debates, scrutiny and amendment. The complete process is explained below:

White paper: This contains the government's idea for a bill. It is written to allow discussion and consultation with interested parties before the idea becomes a bill.

First reading: The bill is read or introduced to parliament without a debate or vote taking place.

Second reading: The bill is debated and must be approved in a vote to proceed.

Committee stage: The bill goes through detailed scrutiny by an all-party Public Bill Committee and amendments are made, if required.

Report stage: The whole House of Commons considers any amendments made by the Committee and can accept, alter or reject them.

Third reading: The amended bill is debated but cannot be amended again at this stage. A vote is taken on whether to accept the amended bill.

If the amended bill passes this stage it goes to the House of Lords, where the whole process is repeated. If the Lords amend the bill even more, it is returned to the Commons for approval; at this point, the amendments made by the Lords may be accepted, rejected or changed by the House of Commons. This can lead to what is known as 'parliamentary ping-pong', as a bill is bounced back and forth between the two houses. Ultimately though, if agreement cannot be reached it is the Commons that has the greater power. It can accept the Lords' amendments, drop the bill altogether or invoke the Parliament Act.

Once the various stages of the bill's passing through parliament have taken place there is then a final vote by MPs on whether to pass the finalised bill on to royal assent and therefore to become an Act of Parliament.

The two most important stages in the passage of a bill are the second reading and the committee stage. During the second reading, the principle of the bill is debated and at this stage it is vulnerable to being thrown out after a vote by the House. At the committee stage, the Public Bill Committee – which is made up of a majority of government MPs and may include party whips – can usually ensure a safe passage for the bill. By having this majority on the committee the government is usually able to squeeze through its bill with minimal changes. As we see later, the size of the government's majority is a key aspect of getting its proposed bill through parliament safely.

Show your understanding

Create detailed diagrams showing all of the different parts of the UK Parliament and also a diagram showing the route a bill takes as it passes through parliament.

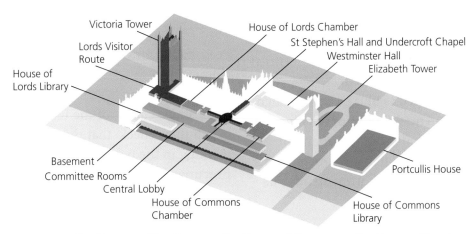

Figure 6.2 **The Houses of Parliament, the House of Commons, the House of Lords, Westminster Hall and the committee rooms**

The House of Commons

Known as the lower chamber, the House of Commons is where most of the high-profile activity takes place in parliament. In this chamber all elected Members of Parliament work for their constituents and hold the government to account. Since 2010 there have been 650 MPs representing the constituencies of the entire United Kingdom although this number has fluctuated in the past and will likely do so in the future due mainly to population changes. This is a form of indirect democracy and in essence ensures that all citizens are represented in parliament. The main roles of the House of Commons can be summed up in the following ways:

- the passing of legislation
- scrutiny of those in power.

The passing of legislation

As shown above, the House of Commons plays a key role in the passing of legislation. In fact, it is the dominant chamber given that the government itself usually holds the balance of power in the chamber. Following the 2015 General Election, the Conservative Party held the balance of power as they had a majority of MPs (331). This gave them the most MPs which in turn meant that under normal circumstances they would not only have a majority of MPs in the chamber but also on many of the committees that work on the government's bills that pass through parliament. The government can therefore rely on their own MPs to help push through their plans.

The vast majority of bills that are processed through parliament are introduced by the government. At the beginning of 2016 some of the government bills making their journey through the various stages of scrutiny were the Psychoactive Substances Bill, the Trade Union Bill and the Immigration Bill.

ICT task

Go to http://services.parliament.uk/bills to check on the current status of the bills that are passing through parliament.

Tony Blair's Labour Government was able to pass all government bills between its election in 1997 and 2005 owing to its large majority of MPs. However, the Conservative–Liberal

Democrat Coalition Government suffered a record number of defeats of its bills between 2010 and 2015, perhaps indicative of the fact that it had to share a majority and many disagreements took place as bills passed through parliament. Any potential dissent or rebellion from its own MPs will make the government listen. However, it is likely that any amendments will be agreed before the bill is presented for its first reading.

Private Members' Bills

Apart from government bills, there are limited opportunities for individual MPs to put forward their own ideas. If they receive enough sponsorship, and they are successfully drawn out of a ballot, they might find that their own bill begins its passage through parliament. For the 2015–16 session only 20 Private Members' Bills were drawn for consideration in parliament. Of course, individual MPs do not necessarily have the support of the majority of MPs so more often than not these bills do not make it all the way through parliament. However, there are a number of examples where a Private Member's Bill has made it all the way to become an Act of Parliament.

- Murder (Abolition of the Death Penalty) Act 1965: Introduced by Sydney Silverman, who was the MP for the Nelson and Colne constituency in Lancashire, it effectively ended the death penalty in Great Britain, replacing it with a sentence of life imprisonment.
- Gangmaster (Licensing) Act 2004: Introduced by Jim Sheridan, who was the MP for Paisley and Renfrewshire North. The Act was passed in response to the Morecambe Bay disaster where 21 Chinese migrant workers were left to drown in the rising tides while collecting shellfish. The law made it illegal to operate such activities without a license. The employers of the drowned workers were later prosecuted for manslaughter.

Scrutiny of government actions

Perhaps the most important role of the House of Commons is to scrutinise the work of the government. The MPs in the chamber represent every single citizen of the UK and so on their behalf they 'check' that the government is working in the best interests of all. Therefore, the Executive is accountable to the general public.

There are a number of processes in place in parliament to examine the work of the government. The main way MPs scrutinise policy is through questioning government ministers, debating current issues and policy and the investigative work of committees. The government can publicly respond to explain and justify its policies and decisions.

Questions

MPs can ask questions of government ministers. The majority of questions asked receive written answers, but some are answered orally for around an hour each day from Monday to Thursday on the floor of the House. For example, the Business, Innovation and Skills Minister will answer questions on Tuesdays at 12.15pm. The most high profile of these sessions is Prime Minister's Question Time (PMQs) which takes place each Wednesday at noon for 30 minutes. These sessions provide an opportunity for the shadow opposition ministers and backbench MPs (selected by the speaker) to 'grill' the prime minister or minister about their policies or actions. A large section of this session is given over to the leader of the opposition who will try to expose a policy flaw or failure and challenge the government to answer important questions. A common critique of PMQs is that it can be drawn into an aggressive shouting match with both sides jeering from the back benches. This is known as 'Punch and Judy politics'. Another criticism of PMQs is that it lacks effectiveness with the prime minister only being able to give short answers as time is severely limited. However, it does give MPs direct access to those with the most power in government.

Figure 6.3 **Prime Minister's Question Time**

Debates

At the end of each day's business, the House adjourns or suspends proceedings until the following day's sitting with a half-hour adjournment debate. This gives MPs an opportunity to discuss government policy, proposed new laws and current issues, but also to raise issues of concern and interest to their constituents. These debates are designed to help MPs reach an informed decision on a subject but are often poorly attended. Since 1999 'Westminster Hall' debates have taken place to allow MPs more time to debate big issues. For example, in January 2016 there were debates on issues such as the safety of young offenders in custody and the resettlement of Syrian refugees in the UK. A regular criticism of these debates is that they can often have very low attendance and may not lead to any meaningful changes in government policy.

ICT task

Visit http://calendar.parliament.uk/ to have a look at what has gone on in parliament over the past week or so.

Show your understanding

1 Why is a majority important in the House of Commons?
2 What are some of the government bills currently making their way through parliament?
3 Explain, in detail, the features of a Private Member's Bill.
4 Describe some of the criticisms of ministers' questions and debates.

Select committees

Each government minister is shadowed by an MP from the opposition whose job it is to scrutinise their work, and the work of their department is also checked by a group of MPs. These groups are known as select committees and their role is to scrutinise the work of all major government departments and concentrate on expenditure, policies and administration. Select committees are widely accepted as the most effective means of parliamentary scrutiny of the Executive and the decision-making process. Each has 11 backbench MP members who are elected by their own party. The select committee system allows for the questioning of ministers and forces them to explain themselves.

Issues with select committees

Select committee membership reflects the composition of the House of Commons, so a government with a majority in the House also has a majority on committees. This has led to criticisms from some commentators that these MPs will put their allegiance to the government before the important job of scrutinising the Executive. As some MPs seek promotion through the ranks of their party they may be reluctant to expose malpractice or irregularities in the government of which they wish to be a part. Also, they cannot compel the government to follow their recommendations. This had led some to describe select committees as 'watchdogs without teeth'. However, in 2011 a report found that 40 per cent of committee recommendations are accepted by government and approximately one-third of recommendations for significant policy changes are implemented. Also, committees are said to play an important part in deterring the government from introducing unpopular policy which the committees may expose to the public and thus damage the Executive's reputation. Select committees have also made headline news by scrutinising some very influential people. In July 2011 Rupert and James Murdoch gave evidence to the Culture, Media and Sport Select Committee as it began its investigation into phone hacking; in July 2012 the Barclays chief executive Bob Diamond gave evidence to the Treasury Select Committee as it investigated rate-rigging; and executives from Starbucks, Google and Amazon gave evidence to the Public Account Committee which has led to Google announcing in January 2016 that it will pay £130 million in backdated tax to HMRC.

In 2006, public bills committees were introduced in place of standing committees to scrutinise legislation. Unlike standing committees, they act in a similar way to select committees: they can call forward witnesses to obtain evidence on the bills and request written information from any interested parties, thereby adding 'teeth' to their legislative scrutiny and its potential impact. However, their composition still reflects the proportion of the parties in parliament, meaning that the government retains a majority on each committee – easing the passage of bills.

The Backbench Business Committee gives backbench MPs the power to call for debates in the chamber and in Westminster Hall at least once a week. It is also responsible for parliament's e-petitions website: in an e-petition, any member of the public can highlight an issue and if the petition gains more than 100,000 signatures the committee will hear the argument for it to be debated by MPs. In January 2016, following an e-petition signed by more than 575,000 people, the House of Commons debated on whether to ban American businessman Donald Trump from entering the UK following his proposals to ban Muslims from entering the USA during his presidential campaign. While many MPs did argue for this ban, the majority decided that it was not in the UK's interest to ban Mr Trump.

Case study: Select committee on phone hacking

In 2011 the Culture, Media and Sport Select Committee held an inquiry into allegations made against the *News of the World* newspaper that it had, over a number of years, been hacking into the voicemails of politicians, celebrities and sports stars. Famous people such as singer Charlotte Church, actress Sienna Miller and footballer David Beckham are thought to have had their phones hacked during this period. The committee, chaired by Conservative MP John Whittingdale, included ten other MPs.

The committee called upon *News of the World* owner Rupert Murdoch, his son James Murdoch and chief executive Rebekah Brooks. It was during one of these meetings that a protestor called Jonnie Marbles attacked Rupert Murdoch with a foam pie, which triggered a huge security alert. The protestor shouted that Murdoch was a 'naughty billionaire', indicating that he disapproved of his company's alleged phone-hacking practices. ⇨

Case study continued...

After hearing the three witnesses, including particularly strong questioning from Labour MP Tom Watson, it was revealed that the voicemail of schoolgirl Milly Dowler, who was murdered in 2002, was hacked and her messages listened to while she was missing, which gave false hope to her parents and to the police that she was still alive.

As a result of the investigation the *News of the World* was closed down and Rebekah Brooks lost her job. The committee recommended to the House of Commons that a judicial inquiry should take place into ethics within the media. This was known as the Leveson Inquiry, which has made wide-ranging recommendations, including the creation of an independent body to monitor press standards which should be backed by legislation.

Backbench Business Committee

Set up in June 2010, the aim of the Backbench Business Committee (BBBC) is to give backbench MPs greater control over the Executive. The committee has eight members from across the main political parties. It meets on Tuesdays to consider requests for debates on any subject from MPs. Journalist Quentin Letts has described this process as being like the TV programme *Dragons' Den* with backbench MPs having to pitch issues to the committee. This is seen as being much more open and transparent than the previous system where the government decided on debates and scheduled all business behind closed doors. Thus more power is now with backbench MPs.

Debates initiated by the BBBC

September 2011 Motion calling for the continued deployment of UK armed forces in Afghanistan. This forced the government to allow MPs to vote on this issue, resulting in the eventual withdrawal of UK troops.

January 2013 Motion to reduce the voting age to 16. This was the first time that MPs had voted on this issue and the motion was passed, putting it on the agenda despite government opposition to the idea.

March 2015 Motion to stop the badger cull. This vote signalled cross-party opposition to the government's policy. It forced the government

into taking a stance on the issue and put it into the public agenda.

While the BBBC has ensured that issues important to backbench MPs are put on the agenda there have been a number of criticisms. As the membership of the committee is severely limited, parties outside of the 'big two' usually have only one representative. For the 2015–16 session this was SNP's Peter Wishart; however, he has described the system as 'deficient and unacceptable'. Also, in 2012 the Coalition Government changed the way members are elected. Previously, the whole house elected members but following a 'whipped' vote, and despite the protestations of the committee itself, it is now party whips who select their members. This was seen as demonstration of executive dominance and accusations that the BBBC now offers less robust scrutiny of the work of the government.

Figure 6.4 A Backbench Business Committee meeting

ICT task

Go to https://petition.parliament.uk.

Look at some of the recent open petitions. If a petition has more than 100,000 signatures then the Backbench Business Committee will hear the arguments for it to be scheduled into parliamentary business. Make a short profile of a petition that interests you. If you feel strongly then why not sign it yourself!

Show your understanding

1. Describe the main features of select committees.
2. Explain some of the limitations of select committees.
3. 'The Backbench Business Committee gives backbench MPs more power.' To what extent is this statement accurate?
4. Give details of the select committee on phone hacking.

Reform of the House of Commons

As with any political institution, the House of Commons should constantly look to change for the better, including staying up to date with the way that the public shows their interest with politics and also the accountability of its members. One criticism of the House of Commons is the way that it is perceived by the general public. Its processes are seen as archaic and generally out of step with modern life. To combat this there have been a number of procedural changes brought about by the recommendations of the Wright Committee that were adopted by the Coalition Government of 2010–15. These reforms included giving backbenchers more say in setting the House's agenda and the establishment of the Backbench Business Committee (see page 95). Further

reforms also include the introduction of elections for chairs and members of select committees and also improvements in the petitions system.

While these changes have largely taken place some still think that more changes are needed. For example, in December 2015 the SNP called for electronic voting as under the current arrangements each vote can take up to 20 minutes to process. The SNP has called this a 'waste of time' and called for an end to the 'antiquated Westminster tradition'. When the SNP's 56 MPs were elected in 2015 they caused a great deal of controversy as they broke a number of long-standing rules such as clapping speeches, sitting where traditionally the opposition party would sit, taking 'selfies' and behaving in an unreserved manner. Many commentators have claimed that this was a deliberate strategy to try to encourage debate about modernisation. Lastly, there has been a movement to capitalise on the use of social media platforms such as Twitter by the public. Several House of Commons select committees now use Twitter to invite the public to submit questions to be posed to government ministers and other witnesses called to committee hearings.

Show your understanding

1. Give details of some of the criticisms of the House of Commons.
2. With a partner, list some of the possible ways in which you think parliament could modernise itself. Your teacher may ask you to share these with the class.

The House of Lords

The House of Lords plays a key role in the legislative process. It debates and scrutinises bills as they pass through parliament, helping to ensure that legislation is well drafted and effective. It makes laws, holds the government to account and investigates policy issues. The people who sit in the House of Lords, unlike members of the House of Commons, are not elected and not paid a salary. There are currently around 840 members, known as lords or peers, making the chamber one of the largest legislative bodies in the world after China's National People's Congress. There are three different types of member: life peers, hereditary peers (who have inherited their title through their family and which is given up upon their death) and bishops. The majority of lords are life peers, chosen because of the work they have done throughout their careers. This can include people such as athletes, actors, scientists, doctors, politicians, lawyers and writers. This expertise is seen as a key asset to the parliament.

Lords can also belong to a political party, and some are chosen by the government to work in and represent one of their departments. For example, in David Cameron's 2015 Government Baroness Stowell and Baroness Anelay were both members of the Cabinet. In terms of party affiliation, almost two-thirds of the peers belong to the Conservative, Labour or Liberal Democrat parties, however, lords prefer to be independent of a political party and are known as crossbenchers. Key to this is the fact that peers are appointed for life and do not need to fight elections. They therefore do not have to follow a particular party line and so can debate and vote freely without outside influence. The House of Lords is seen as being less partisan than the Commons. However, this is also seen as a weakness as peers are not accountable in the same way as their counterparts in the Commons and are not 'judged' by the public via a general election.

Criticisms of the Lords

The House of Lords is a controversial issue in UK politics. While many would argue that it is a unique institution that plays an integral part in scrutiny and the decision-making process, others would argue that it is out-of-step with modern democracy. David Cameron was accused of 'cronyism' after the appointment of 45 new peers in August 2015 as these appointments included 26 former Tory ministers and aides. The SNP, which campaigns for an end to the House of Lords, commented that the appointments 'were a sorry list of rejected politicians, cronies and hangers-on with big chequebooks'. The appointments included former Conservative MP Douglas Hogg who was found, in the expenses scandal of 2009, to have claimed parliamentary expenses for getting the moat at his manor house cleaned.

In addition there is a disproportionately large number of peers with backgrounds in finance and banking and well over a quarter of peers reside primarily in London or the south-east. The sheer number of peers has also led to criticism with peers such as Baroness Deech claiming that there were too many people trying to get their voice heard and that some members have to queue for two hours to be able to get their oral question tabled.

The cost of the House of Lords has also opened it up to criticism. Peers can claim £300 per day for carrying out parliamentary work in the chamber and £150 for work away from Westminster. According to the House of Lords Annual Report the annual operating cost for running the Lords for 2014–15 was £94.4 million; more than £20 million of this was spent on members' allowances and expenses.

Lastly, there are also 26 Lords Spiritual within the chamber who are representatives of the Church of England. Many commentators have argued that religion has no place in politics and that this is not representative of a multi-faith and increasingly secular modern Britain.

Figure 6.5 **Michelle Mone, Scottish businesswoman made a peer by David Cameron in 2015**

Making laws

Nearly all bills have to pass through both the Commons and the Lords prior to becoming Acts of Parliament. Bills (or draft laws) are debated and scrutinised in both houses.

Legislation takes up about 60 per cent of the House of Lords' time, and members are involved throughout the process of proposing, revising and amending legislation. Some bills introduced by the government begin in the Lords in order to spread the workload between the two houses; however, the most important bills start in the House of Commons. The House of Lords is well known for the intensity of its scrutiny, often taking an exhaustive line-by-line approach to the detail of a bill, working to highlight potential problems to try to make better and more effective law. It can amend bills and return them to the Commons for consideration and debate. While any amendments the Lords make may be disregarded by the House of Commons, they do delay the legislative process and force the government and House of Commons to rethink the bill and perhaps come up with alternative amendments. The Parliament Acts of 1911 and 1949 restrict the Lords by limiting its power of delay to a maximum of one year, or one month for financial bills. Traditionally the Lords has not stood in the way of financial bills; however, on 26 October 2015 the House of Lords voted to

Case study: Working tax credits

In a dramatic assertion of its authority, the House of Lords defeated the Conservatives over the planned tax credit cuts. Peers voted in favour of a Labour motion, which demanded full compensation for the low-paid for at least three years, by 289 to 272. An earlier motion, delaying the cuts until the government responds to the Institute for Fiscal Studies' (IFS) assessment, was also approved by 307 to 277. The IFS warned that the cuts would cost three million families an average of £1,000 a year even after taking into account the new 'national living wage' and planned increases in the personal tax allowance. Under the Tories' plan, the earnings level at which tax credits start to be withdrawn would be reduced from £6420 to £3850 from April 2016.

The government avoided complete defeat – the Liberal Democrats' 'fatal motion' was rejected by 310 to 99. Peers overrode the constitutional convention that the Lords does not oppose the government on financial matters.

The failure of the Tories to include the tax credit cuts in their manifesto, and the use of a statutory instrument linked to a welfare act rather than to a finance bill, convinced the Lords that the bill was not covered by the 1911 Parliament Act and so could be rejected. Briefings suggesting that David Cameron could respond by curtailing the Lords' powers, or by flooding the upper chamber with new Conservative members (to give the Tories a majority), only hardened their resolve. Chancellor George Osborne commented that the rejection brought up 'constitutional issues' and David Cameron promised a review into the powers of the House of Lords.

Source: *Adapted from* New Statesman, *26 October 2015*

reject the government's plans to reform Working Tax Credits (see case study on page 98). Following this the government dropped its planned reforms.

(see case study on page 98)

Show your understanding

1 Create a spider diagram detailing some of the key features of the House of Lords.
2 Explain the term 'cronyism' using the House of Lords as a context.
3 What part does the House of Lords play in the passing of legislation?
4 Explain why the working tax credit vote was a 'watershed' moment for the Lords.

Scrutinising the work of the government

Lords check the work of the government by questioning and debating decisions made by ministers and government departments. About 40 per cent of their time is spent on scrutiny.

The House of Lords plays a vital role in scrutinising the work of the government and holding it to account for its decisions and activities. With government ministers sitting in the House and many former ministers, senior politicians and officials among its membership, the House of Lords is well placed to question the government with rigour and insight. Because its members do not represent constituencies and therefore do not need to satisfy the wishes of voters, and are not subject to pressure from whips, they can speak and vote freely on issues.

They can also debate controversial issues that are generally avoided by the House of Commons such as abortion and genetic engineering – topics about which MPs are often afraid of exposing their personal opinions in case it creates conflict with their constituents and parties.

On a daily basis, peers keep a close eye on the government by asking oral and written questions, responding to government statements or debating key issues. In all cases, the government's reply is a matter of public record, meaning that the House of Lords is able to make a significant contribution to improving transparency and the public's understanding of the government's actions.

Questions

Members can ask oral questions on any aspect of the government's activities in the chamber; these are answered by a government minister. While most questions are published in advance, the House has a separate procedure for tabling urgent 'private notice' questions. There is also the opportunity for written questions; these are used more often, and increasingly by members to extract information from the government.

Statements

The government often makes important announcements by means of an oral or written statement to one or both houses of parliament. Following an oral statement to the House of Lords, members are able to question the government minister to raise concerns or seek clarification on any point of policy or fact.

Debates

Debates account for 30 per cent of business in the House of Lords chamber, with members not restricted to debating the legislative programme. They can propose debates on any topic, at the end of which a government minister responds to the questions, concerns and other matters that have been raised.

The professional expertise and specialist knowledge of members are valuable and help to ensure that issues and questions that otherwise might not be highlighted are brought to the

Reforming the House of Lords

Over recent decades there have been a number of reforms to the House of Lords.

House of Lords Act 1999

The Labour Party, under the leadership of Tony Blair, removed all but 92 of the House of Lords hereditary peers. In July 2012 the number had fallen to 89. After this change a commission (a group of selected experts) was set up in 2000, headed by Lord Wakeham. The commission looked at completely reforming the Lords. Since this time successive governments have promised to make changes to the House of Lords but have largely failed. The only major reform to take place has been the movement of the Court of Appeal from the Lords to the UK Supreme Court in 2009.

Following this major reform there have been a number of failed attempts at reforming the Lords. These are:

House of Lords Reform Bill 2012

The coalition agreement following the 2010 General Election included reform of the Lords and in June 2012 the Coalition Government produced a bill recommending the following reforms:

- Reduce the number of peers from 826 members to 450.
- The majority – 80 per cent – of members would be elected.
- But 90 members – 20 per cent – would still be appointed, by an Appointments Commission, on a non-party basis.
- Time-limits – peers would serve a non-renewable 15-year term instead of being members for life.
- A reduced number of bishops – the number of Church of England bishops would be reduced.
- The chamber would still be called the House of Lords but members would not have the title 'Lord'.

This failed to pass through parliament under the 2010–15 Coalition Government, however, following the government's defeat over the working tax credits issues there has been a renewed interest in reforming the Lords.

government's attention. Because of this, debates in the House of Lords are effective in influencing the decision-making process and helping to shape policy and laws. This expertise was illustrated in a recent House of Lords debate on prescription charges in England which included former deans of university medical schools, dentists, former GPs, former consultants, professors of nursing, the president of Mencap and the former director of Age Concern (now Age UK).

Committees in the House of Lords have a different function to those in the Commons. Each Lords committee focuses on a broad subject area rather than a particular government department. The committees also benefit from the specialist knowledge and wide range of experience of their members. This allows for a more rigorous and independent approach to scrutiny.

Why has reform been so problematic?

- MPs feel that if the peers in the Lords were to become elected then this would reduce their own power and the Lords would no longer only be a 'revising chamber'.
- Since the reduction in the number of hereditary peers, many believe that the Lords has become more effective.
- An elected second chamber would remove the relative independence of the Lords and would

see peers pandering for votes and following the party line.

- As part of the legislation process, peers in the House of Lords would have to vote themselves out of position, which is unlikely to happen.
- Many people feel that the time and resources used trying to reform the Lords would be better used in trying to improve the lives of the British public. For example, tackling unemployment or improving living conditions.

Added Value idea

Perhaps your assignment could be based around reforming the House of Lords.

Show your understanding

1 Explain, in detail, why some consider the Lords an effective scrutiniser of government policy.
2 Describe, in detail, the main changes that took place in the Lords under Tony Blair's premiership.
3 Working with a partner, create a table in which some of proposed changes to the Lords are listed alongside the possible problems that may arise from these changes. Be prepared to share your findings with the rest of the class.

The Executive

The UK Executive is made up of three parts as follows:

- the prime minister
- the Cabinet
- the civil service.

The Executive is the key decision-making body in the UK. It has the power, authority and legitimacy to make most of the decisions that affect all of our lives and is the main influence of the direction a country takes. This is primarily done through formulating and implementing policy. The prime minister and the Cabinet are politically motivated and partisan in their decision-making capacity – together they make up the government. The civil service is politically neutral and it is their job to advise the government and carry out their plans.

Role of the prime minister

According to the prime minister's own website, they are head of the UK Government and are ultimately responsible for the policy and decisions of the government. The key roles are overseeing the operation of the civil service, appointing members of the Cabinet/government and being the principal government figure in the House of Commons.

A common misunderstanding is how the prime minister is selected. Unlike the president of the USA, the prime minister is not directly elected. In fact, the prime minister is chosen by the monarch, who through constitutional convention picks the person who has the support of the House of Commons; this is usually the leader of the largest political party in the Commons. It is this majority that allows the prime minister to take the lead in government. The ultimate 'check' on the power of government and the prime minister lies with ordinary MPs. If a prime minster does not have the support of the majority of the House of Commons chamber, the Commons can pass a vote of no confidence, leading to the resignation of the prime minister and the government. This happened to the minority Labour Government of James Callaghan in 1979. In the election that followed, the Conservatives, under Margaret Thatcher, came to power. Labour did not form a government again until 1997, when Tony Blair won with a landslide victory.

Powers of the prime minister

With the role of the prime minister comes several powers that are given in order for them to be able to lead effectively. However, some of these powers will vary depending upon a number of circumstances, many of which are out of the control of the prime minister. This was summed up by former prime minister Harold Macmillan; when asked by a journalist what he most feared he replied 'events, dear boy, events'. Given the events of June 2016, David Cameron might have agreed.

Royal prerogative

The prime minister holds prerogative powers that afford them traditional authority. They are historic powers formally exercised by the monarch acting alone, but which now are exercised by the prime minister. They enable the leader to rule virtually by decree, without the backing of or consultation with parliament.

Some of these powers include:

- the recognition of foreign states
- the declaration of war
- the deployment of armed forces in the UK and abroad
- the making of treaties
- the accreditation of diplomats
- the appointment and dismissal of ministers
- the restructuring of government departments
- the appointment of special advisors
- the issuing and withdrawal of passports
- the granting of honours
- appointments to, and employment conditions of, the civil service
- the calling of elections.*

*limited by fixed-term parliaments

On an individual basis the majority of these powers are administrative but as a collective they make the prime minister the most powerful individual in office.

Show your understanding

1 Describe how a prime minister is selected.
2 Explain what happens to the prime minister in a 'vote of no confidence'.
3 Outline some of the prerogative powers exercised by the prime minister.

Sources and limitations of power

As well as the prerogative powers given to the prime minister, their position within parliament gives them a number of additional powers. What is significant about these extra powers is that they are subject to change. When describing the role of government the famous saying 'a week is a long time in politics' is used regularly and with regards to the amount of power a prime minister can yield it is particularly pertinent.

Majority party leadership

As the leader of the largest party in the House of Commons, the prime minister usually has a majority and therefore is able to implement the proposed government legislation; however, this varies depending on general election results. The Labour leader Tony Blair commanded great power and authority in his first two terms in office from 1997 to 2005, but this ebbed away from 2005 to 2007, when he left office earlier than intended. The then Conservative leader David Cameron, in his first term from 2010 to 2015, had to form a coalition with the Liberal Democrats to establish a Commons majority but lost the support of some MPs because of the compromises he made. In his most recent term he commanded a slim majority in the Commons; however, this means that he was at risk of losing power if a small number of Conservative MPs defied the whip. Indeed it was widely rumoured that Cameron allowed the European Union referendum to take place due to pressure from a fairly small group of Conservative MPs, showing that his power was limited.

Image and popularity

A key source of prime ministerial power is their popularity among the general public. Prime ministers attract much media attention and live with a high degree of public scrutiny as spokesperson for the government. They also provide national leadership at home and on the international stage, leading the nation in times of crisis and emergency. They sit down with other world leaders and attend high-profile meetings, such as at the G8 and EU summits. They are directly involved in foreign policy, and it is the prime minister who negotiates treaties. A popular and well-liked prime minister will have the support of the people and this will be reflected in high ratings in the polls. David Cameron consistently had higher approval ratings than other high-profile Conservatives and Opposition leaders, especially when it comes to people's perception of him as an effective leader. The key to this is that the popularity of the leader will directly affect the popularity of the party and so MPs will support a leader who is seen as an electoral asset as they stand a better chance of retaining their status as MPs in future elections.

High-profile colleagues

In theory, the prime minister has the ability to create a Cabinet in their own image. In reality, a prime minister's power within the Cabinet is limited by a need to assuage the ambitions of party colleagues. Senior party members and those who have been loyal and show potential may expect to be included in the government regardless of their own personal political views.

The prime minister is also restricted by the pool of MPs that is available; while it is their only resource, it can also provide obstacles. Subsequently, the prime minister may be pushed into offering positions to potential rivals and opponents: these people may be less trouble inside the Cabinet, where they are bound by the convention of collective responsibility, rather than outside it on the back benches, where they could stir up dissent and be a focus for rebels should a policy be controversial.

Margaret Thatcher, Conservative prime minister from 1979 to 1990, was regarded as a strong and effective leader. Yet 'the Iron Lady', as she was known, was effectively forced out of office by her Cabinet colleagues in November 1990, thus demonstrating the limitation of the office of the prime minister. Tony Blair was regarded as an effective leader, winning three elections in a row.

Prime Minister Cameron had trouble with the right of his party in his first year in office. This was because of his support on giving some prisoners the vote, his Home Secretary's liberal views on law and order, and the cuts to the defence budget while the international aid budget was maintained. In fact, Cameron saw more of his own MPs rebel and faced more revolts in his first year in office than Tony Blair did during the whole of his first term.

Cameron brought the former Conservative leader William Hague into the Cabinet as Foreign Secretary in 2010 to shore up his own position, and then was reluctant to oust him when things started to go wrong. Mr Hague faced criticism over his handling of the crisis in Libya in 2011. Cameron also made high-profile Conservative Boris Johnson a part-time member of the Cabinet, given his power in the party and his former role as Mayor of London. Prime Minister Theresa May appointed Mr Johnson as Foreign Secretary in her first cabinet.

Events

Several key events limited Gordon Brown's power as prime minister and eventually led to his defeat at the polls in 2010. For example, the global financial crisis, the unexpected backlash over the Gurkha resettlement issue and the damaging MPs' expenses controversies, followed by the resignations of several key Cabinet members, were just some of the events during his premiership that indicated his dwindling power and support. Under Cameron's leadership there had been a few events such as the migrant crisis and the independence and European referenda that had a draining effect on his premiership. However, some would argue that the April 2016 revelation that he profited £30,000 from a tax-haven scheme in Panama in 2009 also had a negative impact on his power. He effectively resigned from office after the June 2016 EU 'Leave' result.

The Opposition

The 'official opposition' is the largest minority party, and its main purpose is to oppose the government of the day. This can be both a source of and a drain on prime ministerial power. As leader of the largest opposition party (Labour), Jeremy Corbyn was elected in 2015 as Opposition leader in the Commons. The leader of the Opposition picks a 'Shadow Cabinet' to follow and scrutinise the work of each government department and the policies being developed in their specific areas. A weak opposition leader can help elevate the prime minster, making them look even more statesman-like; however, as Cameron was to Gordon Brown, a strong opposition leader can weaken the image of the prime minister.

Power of patronage

The prime minister also has the power to be involved in appointing people to important positions outside the government. For example, they can make political nominations to the House of Lords and are allowed to approve one person for a top ecclesiastical appointment in the Church of England. They also have the key role in the 'new year's honours list' in which the monarch awards people for their service to Britain through knighthoods, MBEs and CBEs.

In December 2015 Cameron was criticised for awarding mainly Tory allies and donors in the list. Australian Lynton Crosby was awarded a knighthood for 'political service' after being the chief election strategist for Cameron during the 2010 election. Following the 'cash for honours' scandal in which Tony Blair was questioned by police and several lords were cautioned and investigated, many political commentators have suggested that this power has been weakened. For example, the Conservatives' largest ever single donor Lord Ashcroft, who is estimated to have given the party more than £8 million, abstained from any further patronage after a public spat with Cameron.

Show your understanding

1 Explain the importance of a parliamentary majority for the prime minister.
2 What evidence is there to suggest that 'image' is important for the prime minister?
3 Explain why having high-profile colleagues can be both advantageous and damaging to prime ministerial power.
4 Describe some of the controversies surrounding the power of patronage.
5 'A week is a long time in politics.' To what extent may this be true in relation to prime ministerial power?

Recent prime ministers

Tony Blair (1997–2007)

Tony Blair led the Labour Party to a landslide victory in 1997 and 2001 giving him huge power and achieving super majorities on both occasions. He had a celebrity-like status and was often courted by the media. Famously he hosted events in Downing Street to which he invited popular actors and musicians, which enhanced his image. In addition he featured as a special guest on TV shows such as the comedy programme *The Catherine Tate Show* as part of a Comic Relief Special. However, he only managed a much reduced majority in 2005 as his popularity began to dwindle due primarily to his government's decision to invade Iraq and the subsequent failure to find any weapons of mass destruction, which had been their justification for entering the conflict. Tony Blair was seen as the first prime minister to take on a presidential style of leadership due to the importance placed on his image and his micromanagement style.

Figure 6.6 Tony Blair with Noel Gallagher from Oasis in Downing Street

Gordon Brown (2007–10)

Gordon Brown began his premiership with a huge disadvantage in that he had not led the party to success in a general election. Despite dealing decisively with the banking crisis of 2008 and 2009 and being a leading voice in the G20 summit on the issue, domestically he did not receive the credit he perhaps deserved. He failed to ever have the legitimacy of the office and also came up against a charismatic opposition leader in Cameron which further damaged his image and popularity. Brown was widely disliked and lampooned at the hands of the media. His perceived lack of charisma and personality resulted in his ratings plummeting throughout 2009 and up to the election in 2010 and this resulted in a lack of support from some Labour MPs who felt he damaged their own chances of re-election.

Figure 6.7 Gordon Brown with his family leaving Downing Street following defeat in the 2010 general election

David Cameron (2010–16)

Cameron was dealt an unusual hand in his first term in that he was the prime minister of a coalition government. This constrained his power in several ways. He had always to consult Deputy Prime Minister Nick Clegg on the direction of government, he had Liberal Democrat members in his Cabinet and also he had to manage disappointed members of his own party who did not want to concede points to their coalition party. Cameron was able to successfully navigate this difficult task due to his background in public relations and his role as facilitator. Following a majority win in 2015 he maintained this approach ⇨

but had to concede his power slightly after he announced that he would not stand for a third term in 2020. Immediately after the 'Leave' victory in the EU Referendum, he announced that he would resign as prime minister following the appointment of a new leader of the Conservative Party. As such, he resigned on 13 July 2016 and Theresa May became the new Conservative leader and the new prime minister.

Theresa May (2016–?)

Time will only tell what unique style Theresa May will bring to the office of prime minister. She began decisively by sacking George Osborne from the Chancellor of the Exchequer position and also dismissed Michael Gove from the position of Justice Minister.

Figure 6.8 David Cameron during the 2016 EU Referendum campaign

Table 6.3 **Three prime ministers compared**

Blair		Brown		Cameron	
Strategy	Directive	**Strategy**	Indecisive	**Strategy**	Facilitator
Tactics	PMs office the centre of power	**Tactics**	A limited return to the Cabinet being the centre of power	**Tactics**	Stable, managerial, careful coalition management
Context	Large majority, weak opposition, strong economy	**Context**	Economic crisis, weak party, opposition renewal	**Context**	Coalition government, deficit reduction, weak majority, migrant crisis and Europe

Source: *Politics Review*

Power of appointment/dismissal

The power to appoint and dismiss government ministers – especially Cabinet ministers – is arguably where most of the prime minister's regular power lies. It is the prime minister who decides which MPs to reward or punish by appointing them to specific posts and including them in or excluding them from the Cabinet. This power to 'hire or fire' includes the power to 'reshuffle' (or refresh) the make-up of the Cabinet or government whenever they deem it necessary. This can allow the prime minister to create a Cabinet of loyal supporters; however, in reality it is best to consider the selection carefully, paying close attention to people's

ambitions. If someone is overlooked for promotion they can become resentful, and it is important for the prime minister to retain the support and loyalty of all their MPs. In his memoirs Tony Blair calls those left out as the 'ejected, dejected and rejected' who eventually come to 'resent you'.

Blair was forced to include Gordon Brown in the Cabinet as Chancellor of the Exchequer from 1997 until his own resignation in 2007, and was effectively powerless to remove him. This was a tactical decision by Blair who recognised that Brown was a hugely influential figure within the party and outside of the Cabinet he could cause chaos for his leadership.

Cameron in his role as prime minister of a coalition government conceded some of this power to the Deputy Prime Minister and Liberal Democrat leader Nick Clegg. Clegg had sole charge over the appointments of Liberal Democrat ministers. With regards to his own Conservative ministers Cameron appointed close allies, such as George Osborne as Chancellor of the Exchequer, but also appointed more controversial figures in the party such as Dr Liam Fox as Defence Secretary. Dr Fox was seen as having far right views over issues such as Europe and so this was a tactical decision by Cameron. In addition, influential party figures such as former leaders William Hague (Foreign Secretary) and Iain Duncan Smith (Work and Pensions Secretary) were brought in to ensure party unity behind the prime minister. Following the 2015 General Election Cameron maintained much of the status quo. However, Mayor of London and political rival Boris Johnson was given a special invitation to the 'political Cabinet', meaning that he would attend some Cabinet meetings but not take a direct part in decision making. Many saw this as an attempt by Cameron to keep Johnson's backbench supporters under his control.

Cabinet chairperson

The prime minister chairs Cabinet meetings, and in so doing has the power to set the agenda and determine what is discussed and – in some cases more importantly – what is not discussed. They also control the pace and direction of the meetings and sum up the 'sense' of what took place.

Under Tony Blair the Cabinet met infrequently. Cabinet meetings tended to be short and informal meetings to discuss the business of the day, involving round the table stock-take reports from the various government departments, which lasted no more than 40 minutes.

Under Cameron, Cabinet government rose in importance because of the need for collegiality

and consultation to make the coalition work. However, this arrangement put the convention of collective responsibility under strain as government members were forced to support policies in public that they had opposed in their manifestos. For example, Nick Clegg later admitted that he 'should have been more careful' about signing the pre-election pledge to oppose any increase in tuition fees. Cameron overcame natural divisions in the Cabinet by setting up the 'Quad' which was informal meetings between the four most influential members of the coalition Cabinet. Cameron, George Osborne, Nick Clegg and Danny Alexander would meet prior to Cabinet meetings to iron out any issues that might be contentious and this was critical to ensure stability.

From 2015 Cameron had the benefit of an all-Conservative Cabinet but still had to carefully manage the various characters to ensure he remained powerful. His decision to hold a referendum on EU membership led to his resignation in 2016 after the public voted to leave.

Show your understanding

1 Create detailed profiles on each of the last three prime ministers.
2 Explain why being Cabinet chairperson enhances the prime minister's power.
3 Explain the function of the 'Quad'.

12-mark question
Analyse the powers of the prime minister.

The Cabinet

The Cabinet is essentially a government committee that is chaired by the prime minister. Every other member is in charge of a government department and with this position a minister is given the title of Secretary of State, a large pay increase and huge influence over the way that the country is run. It is often seen as the pinnacle in a career in UK politics and these positions are coveted by ambitious MPs. The Cabinet meets once per week to discuss the key events that are taking place in the governance of these departments. The Cabinet is usually made up of between 20 and 25 ministers but this is at the discretion of the prime minister and they have full power over the appointments to these posts.

This group of MPs is the public face of government and so it is important to support its collective decisions. It is a case of 'united we stand, divided we fall': a divided Cabinet is a serious bleeding of prime ministerial power. The table in the Cabinet room is deliberately oval-shaped so that the prime minister, who sits in the centre of one of the long sides, can see the faces and body language of all the Cabinet and so spot any small signs of loyalty or dissent.

The prime minister has traditionally been referred to as *primus inter pares*, which means 'first among equals', and demonstrates that they are a member of the collective decision-making body of the Cabinet, rather than an individual who has powers in their own right. The prime minister is first among equals simply in recognition of the responsibility held for appointing and dismissing all the other Cabinet members. This can make ministers feel that they are beholden to the prime minister and owe them their loyalty.

The prime minister chairs the meeting and sets its agenda; they also decide who speaks around the Cabinet table and sum up at the end of each item. It is this summing up that becomes government policy, with all members being collectively responsible for all decisions and policies. The secretary of the Cabinet is responsible for preparing records of its

discussions and decisions. As the complexity of government decision making has evolved, more agents have become involved. Prime ministers are now more likely to consult with external think tanks, Cabinet committees and special advisers before making decisions. For example, the Cabinet Office Briefing Room A (COBRA), which has both ministers and non-government officials, takes decisions on national security in emergency situations. This leads to the perception that the Cabinet may be less important than it once was, and is only there to rubber-stamp decisions that have already been made or to present government policy and decisions.

Collective responsibility

Collective responsibility is at the heart of Cabinet government. The Cabinet tries to reach decisions on the basis that, as members of the government, ministers are collectively responsible and have to publicly support and defend those decisions regardless of their personal opinions – or resign. This again gives the prime minister great power as any Cabinet disagreements are usually kept in-house and are not made public. However, when a Cabinet minister does resign over a disagreement with government policy it can be hugely embarrassing for the prime minister. Under Blair, Robin Cook and Clare Short resigned from the Labour Government in 2003 over the war in Iraq; meanwhile, in 2009 Communities Secretary Hazel Blears resigned after publicly criticising the government's performance, as did Work and Pensions Secretary James Purnell, who felt he could no longer publicly support Gordon Brown and called for the prime minister to stand aside.

Under Cameron there were a couple of high-profile resignations due to disagreement on policy. Baroness Warsi, who was the first ever female Muslim Cabinet minister, resigned in 2014 over disagreements with the government's foreign policy. She publically announced her resignation on Twitter stating that 'with deep regret I have this morning written to the Prime Minister & tendered my resignation. I can no longer support Govt policy on #Gaza'. In March 2016, Work and Pensions Secretary Iain Duncan Smith resigned from the Cabinet, as he felt his position was threatened by the planned changes to disability benefits brought forward by Chancellor George Osborne in the March 2016 budget. The proposed changes were subsequently dropped. However, Cameron was largely able to successfully iron out disagreements in the Cabinet, which enhanced his reputation as a shrewd communicator. In addition, several ministers such as Liam Fox, Maria Miller and Chris Huhne have resigned over personal scandals. On the face of it this may not have limited Cameron's power but as he appointed these ministers it reflected badly on his ability to appoint suitable ministers for the top positions in government.

Such was the division within the Conservative Party and Cabinet over the EU that David Cameron felt obliged to drop collective responsibility over this issue. Six Cabinet members, if one includes Boris Johnson, supported leaving the EU and were allowed to campaign for an exit.

Cabinet committees

Much of the work of Cabinet is delegated to committees. These committees can reduce the burden on the Cabinet by enabling collective decisions to be made by a smaller group of ministers who are able to deal more efficiently with the large volume of government business. Often, the need for quick decision making means that it is not possible to involve the whole Cabinet in many policy decisions. Consequently, the prime minister selects a smaller group of around four or five ministers to form committees; they can come up with policies and present them to the prime minister and Cabinet more quickly.

Individual ministerial responsibility

Individual ministerial responsibility ensures that ministers are accountable to parliament and the public for their own personal conduct and that of the department they run. This doctrine implies that ministers are ultimately accountable and should take full responsibility for their own or their department's mistakes and resign. This is even expected of them should the mistake not be their own but that of civil servants in the department in order to maintain the anonymity of civil servants.

For example, in 2010 David Laws became the shortest-serving Cabinet member in modern British political history. The Liberal Democrat MP served as chief secretary to the Treasury for just 16 days before it was discovered that he had claimed expenses that he should not have claimed, so he resigned. He said, 'the public is entitled to expect politicians to act with a sense of responsibility for our actions … I do not see how I can carry out my crucial work on the budget and spending review while I have to deal with the private and public implications of recent revelations'.

Show your understanding

1 Describe the main features of the Cabinet.
2 Explain in detail the terms *'primus inter pares'* and collective responsibility.

The civil service

The civil service helps the government of the day to develop and deliver its policies as effectively as possible. The role of the senior civil service is to offer impartial advice to ministers and inform them of the possible consequences and the potential advantages and disadvantages of their actions or decisions. Civil servants are permanent in the sense that their appointment means they cannot be removed by a dissatisfied minister or following a general election. This continuity of tenure allows them to build up experience and expertise that is usually lacking in a minister, and enables them to offer genuinely neutral advice without the worry of any personal political implications. It also means that, because of the high turnover of government ministers, they are likely to serve many ministers. It has been calculated that the average tenure of a government minister in the Blair government was just 1.3 years, with junior ministers being moved more or less on an annual basis.

Many commentators would argue that civil servants are essential for an effective government as they are neutral. This means the advice they give to Cabinet secretaries must be free from any bias towards the fortunes of one political party and must not be influenced by any political ideology. Senior civil servants are not allowed to participate in any party politics and when a government changes, these civil servants will serve their new employers in exactly the same ways as the previous ones. Also, civil servants work in the background of governance. They are not in the public limelight and should not take individual responsibility for any actions taken. Ultimately, the Secretary of State has full responsibility for the work of each government department. This means that civil servants are not under the same political pressures as government ministers and can carry out their duties 'above' politics.

Former Cabinet Office minister Francis Maude is an open critic of the civil service. He argues that given their position at the heart of decision making they should be held more accountable. He argues that civil servants question government ministers too much when it is not their business to do so, that their permanent position means that many feel above criticism and expect government ministers to 'carry the can' for errors that they have made. At the 2014 Conservative Party conference Maude said 'I'm sometimes accused of wanting to "politicise" the civil service. I don't want that. It isn't political to expect civil servants to implement the will of the elected government. It's called democracy.'

Riddell Report

In 2013 political commentator Peter Riddell wrote a report for the Institute for Government on the changing relationship between civil servants and government ministers. His report was particularly critical of the increasing politicisation of the civil service. He found that:

- Civil servants are increasingly under pressure and their anonymity is being challenged by often appearing in public in front of Commons select committees.
- When mistakes are made, ministers are increasingly shifting the blame on to civil servants rather than taking full accountability.
- There has been more interference with the hiring and firing of civil servants. Traditionally civil servants are appointed as permanent employees and should be awarded promotions on merit rather than political grounds.

Case study: Sir Robert Devereux

In 2013, following a delay in the implementation of the government's new universal tax system, a row broke out between ministers and their civil servants. Work and Pensions Secretary Iain Duncan Smith publically blamed his permanent secretary Sir Robert Devereux for the mistakes leading to the delay. Many accused Mr Smith of hiding behind his civil servant and were critical of the Cabinet as it backed the actions of the minister. Britain's most senior civil servant Sir Jeremy Heywood (the Cabinet secretary) publically came out in defence of Devereux. The principles of anonymity and accountability were completely shattered by this public spat.

Source: Politics Review, *January 2016*

Special advisers

A special adviser or 'spad' is a minister's principal political confidant, advising, liaising and most famously spinning the party view. When you read in a newspaper comments by an 'aide' to a minister or 'sources close to the minister', that's usually the spad commenting.

Spads hold a privileged and special role in government. Like civil servants, they are paid by the taxpayer but they do not need to be politically neutral. Whereas civil servants offer neutral advice to ministers, spads offer political advice. Their key purpose has been described as 'devilling' or 'squirrelling' away at all government policy and communications to ensure that it complies with or 'toes' the appropriate party or political line. Whereas civil servants must not engage in any political activity that could be interpreted as compromising their independence and must promise to act impartially, spads are openly political but cannot override advice from officials that they find unpalatable.

With the exception of the prime minister and their deputy, Cabinet ministers generally have just two spads each. Former Prime Minister David Cameron approved the appointment of every special adviser. In his biography, Tony Blair admits to having accumulated 70 at one point – 'considered by some to be a bit of a constitutional outrage', he adds. However, he saw them as essential to speeding up the process of political decision making and a sensible way of enlarging the scope of available advice. This famously is referred to as Blair's **Sofa Government** in reference to the fact that there was a string of accusations that he made many important decisions with his backroom team as opposed to his Cabinet colleagues.

Unlike the appointment of civil servants, there is no merit-based process to that of the spad. Ministers simply choose whoever they reckon is best for the job; the only restriction is that the prime minister must approve every appointment.

However, many feel as though spads have too much political influence on ministers. For example, there was concern over the influence that spad Dominic Cummings had on former Education Secretary Michael Gove over educational reforms that were seen as too radical by some. David Cameron's appointment of Christopher Lockwood to his team of advisors was seen as an example of cronyism and creating an 'inner political circle' which is not conducive to open government.

Conflict between spads and civil servants

In September 2001 Jo Moore, the spin doctor of Stephen Byers, minister for the Department of Transport, Local Government and the Regions (DTLR), had faced calls for her resignation when it became known that she had advised 'burying bad news' by issuing departmental press releases immediately after the 9/11 terrorist attacks.

Byers protected her, but Moore was forced to offer a public apology for her behaviour. Relations between Moore and the senior civil servants within the department, including the Director of ⇨

Communications, Martin Sixsmith, were strained and hostile. In February 2002, more allegations against Jo Moore were leaked and she agreed to resign after Byers promised that Sixsmith would also be forced to resign.

Byers informed the House of Commons that he had accepted Sixsmith's resignation.

This was untrue because Sixsmith had not offered his resignation. Byers was forced to resign because he had told the House a direct lie. As the *Sunday Times* stated, the whole affair highlighted 'a ministry in chaos and a government staffed by apparatchiks who had lost contact with the truth'.

Show your understanding

1 Describe in detail the role of the civil service.
2 Outline the key criticisms of the civil service.
3 'The civil service has power without accountability.' To what extent is this statement accurate?
4 Describe in detail the role of special advisors.
5 Explain why many political commentators criticise the role of special advisors.

20-mark questions

1 To what extent can parliament effectively scrutinise the work of the Executive?
2 'The powers of the prime minister are limited by parliament and the Cabinet.' Discuss.

The Judiciary

Parliament is sovereign. It is the chief legislative body and is where the major decisions about the UK are made. In contrast to the USA where the courts can strike down laws that are deemed to be unconstitutional, the UK's courts can only dream of such power as the UK has an uncodified constitution (see Chapter 2).

Arguments for court interference

The courts only have the power to rule on laws passed by parliament and often only on individual cases that they may see as being unlawful; however, the government can overrule the Judiciary through an Act of Parliament. An example of this is anti-terrorism laws. In 2001 the courts ruled that part IV of the Anti-terrorism, Crime and Security Act 2002 was unlawful and ordered the release of suspects held without trial. However, the Government created and passed through parliament the Prevention of Terrorism Act in 2006 which allows the Home Secretary to impose 'control orders' that effectively allow the holding of suspects.

Many argue that the Judiciary plays an important role in the running of the country as it has huge experience, is unbiased and need only focus on enforcing the law fairly. It also plays a key role in protecting the rights of the individual as was shown in 2011 when courts prevented the deportation of 177 foreign criminals on the grounds that their right to family entitled them to remain in the UK. When Prime Minister Theresa May was Home Secretary, she accepted that government ministers' power needs to be 'reviewed and restrained' by the Judiciary.

Arguments against court interference

The key argument against judges interfering in governance is that they undermine the sovereignty of the parliament. After all, MPs who create and process new laws through parliament are elected representatives and so have legitimacy to make laws that affect all citizens. Judges are unelected and often belong to an elite middle-class background and so have no legitimacy to interfere in the political realm. Perhaps the greatest impact on the sovereignty of parliament has been the introduction of the European Convention on Human Rights (ECHR) into UK law through the 1998 Human Rights Act. It gave judges unprecedented powers over areas such as immigration, penal policy, security, privacy and freedom of expression. This, along with the expansion of judicial review (see the case study on Bedroom Tax) and the impact of EU legislation, has resulted in many government decisions being overruled by the Judiciary – such as undermining parliament's attempts to set minimum sentences for certain crimes, introducing privacy laws by the backdoor and attempts to publically criticise the Government over its decision to deport hate preacher Abu Qatada and the freezing of assets belonging to suspected terrorists.

Case study: Bedroom tax challenge

The Government's so-called 'Bedroom Tax' policy has been declared discriminatory and unlawful by the Court of Appeal. Judges made the decision following a legal challenge against the Government by a domestic violence victim and the family of a disabled teenager. The charge, which takes the form of a reduction in housing support for people with more than a certain number of bedrooms, was introduced in April 2013 to encourage people to move out of homes they are 'under occupying'. It has since been criticised for causing poverty, disproportionally affecting the disabled, and hitting people who have nowhere suitable to move to.

The Department for Work and Pensions said it would appeal the decision in the Supreme Court – the UK's highest and final appellate court. One of the two successful appeals was brought by a woman identified as 'A' who had been a victim of domestic violence. Her home has been specially adapted to include a panic room. Her lawyers claimed the policy discriminated against her because she would have to leave a room that had been adapted for her safety. Wheelchair users and disabled people have made similar claims.

The second successful appeal was brought by Paul and Susan Rutherford on behalf of their severely disabled grandson Warren. Warren suffers from a rare genetic disorder and requires 24-hour care because he cannot walk, talk or feed himself. The couple was hit by the Bedroom Tax because they have a room that is used for overnight carers and storing specialist medical equipment.

The court found the policy's impact on disabled children was contrary to the European Convention on Human Rights. Both appeals were being considered by the Court of Appeal because they had been rejected by the High Court.

Source: *Adapted from the* Independent, *27 January 2015*

Show your understanding

Create a spider diagram detailing the view that the Judiciary can enhance but also interfere with government decision making.

7 Pressure groups

What is a pressure group?

A pressure group usually takes the form of an organisation of like-minded people who want to influence decision makers such as government and other large organisations. Pressure groups aim to influence decision makers by drawing attention to specific issues or specific groups of people. They ultimately hope to influence the behaviour of large organisations, and with relation to influencing the government, hope to make an impact on the formation of legislation, the passing of bills and the amendment of existing laws. Pressure groups feel that they will have more success in pressuring the government as a group rather than individuals. These groups can vary in size from a small group of locals protesting about changes to their local area up to multinational organisations protesting about global issues.

Why do people join a pressure group?

Pressure groups do not usually want to be in government or in mainstream politics as they only have an interest in a particular issue or a particular group of people. For some the traditional method of participating in democracy through political parties is not an attractive prospect. They feel that party politics does not address what they consider to be important issues. Pressure groups offer a narrower and more specific focus, usually on a single issue that can seem more important and more appealing to many. As a result we have seen in recent decades a movement away from political party membership towards pressure group membership.

Since the 1960s membership of political parties has been at a steady decline. At just over 1 per cent of the population, membership of political parties in the UK ranks among the lowest in Europe. Many commentators have suggested that public lack of interest in mainstream politics is the main reason for this. An overall lack of trust in politicians and in mainstream politics itself has resulted in some people looking towards pressure groups as a more honest and accessible way to become involved in politics.

What are the aims of pressure groups?

The role of pressure groups in influencing the decision-making process of a democratic system is a hotly debated subject. While some argue that they enhance the democratic process, others argue that they threaten democracy. Part of this debate relates closely to the aims of pressure groups. Many pressure groups have a specific set of aims. Indeed, there are thousands of short-life pressure groups which are usually locally organised and look to influence decision makers about an issue that affects local communities. For example, in early 2015 a group of local residents protested about the T in the Park music festival being moved to Strathallan Castle Estate in Auchterarder and challenged Perth and Kinross Council's decision to award planning permission (see next page). While the protest was ultimately unsuccessful, the group's aims were seen as honest and fair.

STAG

The Strathallan T Action Group (STAG) was created in 2015 by concerned residents living close to the new site for the T in the Park music festival. Primarily they were concerned with the environmental impact of the relocation and also the impact on the wildlife. Initially they challenged the planning permission decision of Perth and Kinross Council on the grounds that the local area could not handle the volume of traffic. As their protest progressed they discovered and filmed a family of osprey birds that had nested in the proposed site. Ospreys are heavily protected and so the police had to become involved. This led to a review of the planning decision; however, the group was ultimately unsuccessful and the festival went ahead.

Million Mask March

The Million Mask March is a global protest organised by 'hacktivist' group Anonymous. In major cities a large number of people gather for the march and wear Guy Fawkes-style masks to protect their identities. The precise reason for the march is up for debate but most recognise that the protesters are protesting against capitalism, against austerity and for the freedom of speech. However, it could even be debated that Anonymous is not even a pressure group as it does not have a particular cause in mind and is based mainly around internet forums. Indeed, the march in November 2015 turned violent and many consider the group to be no more than a nuisance to society that has no real influence on decision makers.

However, other pressure groups have aims that will not be met in the short term. These groups tend to be more disruptive in their methods and at times their aims will conflict with the democratic process. For example, in November 2015 a large protest dubbed the 'Million Mask March' took place in major cities around the world including London (see box). This group was protesting about capitalism and the austerity cuts. While many would sympathise with their cause they will be unlikely to succeed in the short term with their aims. This can lead to frustration and in some instances violence.

Show your understanding

1 Describe some of the key features of a pressure group.
2 Explain, with examples, three reasons why someone would become a member of a pressure group.
3 Explain the link between pressure group aims and likely success.

Cause groups

Members of cause groups usually have a shared belief or view, so groups are set up to promote a specific cause in which members have an interest. A key feature of cause groups is that anyone can become a member. As long as you have an interest in the cause, you can participate fully in its operations. Cause groups can be in existence for a short period or over the longer term. For example, *We Like Milngavie* was a cause group set up with the aim of preventing a huge expansion of a Tesco supermarket in the

Figure 7.1 The 'Million Mask March'

area. It was a temporary group and campaigned while this was an issue, but disbanded after Tesco announced that they were dropping a planned expansion of their store. On the other hand, a cause group such as Age UK, which aims to promote the rights of elderly citizens, has been around for a much longer period.

Sectional groups

Sectional groups are set up to represent and promote the material interests of a specific group of people in society. These groups will be interested in the needs of their members only. The most popular form of sectional group is a trade union, which looks after the interest of workers. For example, the Scottish Secondary Teachers' Association is a trade union that only represents secondary teachers in Scotland and has no interest in promoting any other groups. Only Scottish secondary school teachers can be members and so it is not open to all.

Insider or outsider?

As well as being categorised by what they campaign for, pressure groups can also be categorised by how they go about carrying out their campaigns. Pressure groups can elect to work with the government and hope to curry favour with decision makers; these groups are known as insider groups. However, pressure groups may elect to work against the government and at times may be in conflict with decision makers; these groups are known as outsider groups. It should be noted that an insider group can become an outsider group depending on which political party is in power. Trade unions are a perfect example of such a group. In the period 1997 to 2010, trade unions were an insider group and played an important role in working with the government to improve pay and working

conditions for ordinary workers. The introduction of the national minimum wage, EU working time directives and an expansion of tax credits for those in work all helped to reduce family and child poverty. However, now there is a Conservative Government, trade unions are regarded mainly as obstacles to Conservative policies and as such have little influence on the Government (see case study on page 117).

Insider groups

As mentioned, insider groups work with the government with the hope of persuading them to address the needs of their cause or members. For this arrangement to be successful, insider pressure groups will often need to carry out their campaigns in a professional and organised manner. They will likely campaign through organised meetings and events and may, in fact, 'have the ear' of the government as they are consulted by decision makers.

Insider groups normally represent professional bodies such as law and medicine. As a result they are often regarded as experts in their fields and can in fact be seen as key stakeholders in drafting legislation and so are part of the policy-formation process. In December 2015, the Commons Health Committee used evidence from Professor Sheila Hollins, chair of the British Medical Association's (BMA) Board of Science, who commented that 'Doctors are increasingly concerned about the impact of poor diet, which is responsible for up to 70,000 deaths a year, and has the greatest impact on the NHS budget, costing £6 billion annually.' The Government sought out the recommendations of the BMA as that is the main organisation that represents medical doctors and consultants. Many of these pressure groups are not well known to the general public as they will often seek change 'behind closed doors' in areas that may not be seen as particularly newsworthy.

However, there are limits to the influence of an insider group on government decision making, especially if it disagrees with government policies. Recently, the Conservative Government wished to change the working conditions of all junior doctors in England and Wales, a move opposed by the BMA. With the Government refusing to back down, doctors were forced to take strike action in 2016. This shows that the positions of trade unions can be variable. Traditionally, the BMA were considered an insider group but in recent times, they have positioned themselves on the outside.

Case study: From insider to outsider – again!

As highlighted trade unions are a perfect example of pressure groups whose influence depends on the ideology of the government of the day. Under Conservative Prime Ministers Margaret Thatcher and John Major (1979–97), numerous new laws were passed to curb trade union powers: the crushing of the NUM (National Union of Miners) in the 1980s is probably the best remembered action of the Conservatives. From a highpoint of more than 13 million members in 1979 the figure for trade union membership now stands at less than 7 million.

The Conservative Government of David Cameron wished to further restrict the trade unions through its 2016 new Trade Union Bill.

Key points of the bill

- Before a strike ballot can take place at least half of all members must agree to a ballot – this will delay action and add to the financial costs of organising a strike ballot.
- Unions representing the public sector such as teachers, doctors and train drivers – assuming they reach the 50 per cent figure – require more than 40 per cent of all those eligible to strike to vote in favour. Those who do not vote will be regarded as voting against the strike.
- Unions, even if they meet the new laws, must give substantial notice before taking strike action and employers will be allowed to hire agency workers to break the strike.
- Workers who contribute to their union's political levy, which goes to the Labour Party, would have to opt-in. This will reduce union donations to the Labour Party. In contrast the Conservatives will still receive lavish funds from Big Business.

Union reaction

The headline in the *Sunday Herald* of 7 February 2016 was: *STUC declares war on Tories over law to break unions*. The largest union, Unite, is urging all of Scotland's 630,000 Scottish trade unionists to fight 'outside the law' to scrap the 'malicious' Trade Union Bill. If the Bill is passed, Unite is urging its members to defy the law and take illegal action.

The Scottish Government opposes the Bill but is helpless to stop it as industrial relations is a reserved issue. A spokesperson stated that the 'Trade Union Bill is bad for workers, bad for business and bad for Scotland … It is intent on destroying the effectiveness of trade unions and Scotland's good industrial relations.'

Figure 7.2 **Trade unionists marching against the Bill**

Outsider groups

Whereas some pressure groups may 'have the ear' of the government, many find themselves forced to challenge and at times disrupt the work of government. On many occasions these pressure groups will act out in public to try to draw attention to their cause or issue. At times, this can even become destructive, chaotic and violent, resulting in law-breaking and arrests. This means that they will usually have a negative relationship with government and will be excluded from the policy-making process. It is this exclusion that can lead many groups to take direct action as they feel that their concerns are not being noted by decision makers and so they have to pressure them by bringing publicity to their issue. For example, on 29 November 2015, a group called New Fathers4justice embarrassed the government by breaking into Buckingham Palace and protesting on the roof. This was following a proclamation by David Cameron that he had put in place a step-up in security across all public buildings in the UK following the Paris terrorist attack earlier that month.

Owing to the very public nature of their protests, outsider pressure groups will often have a much bigger public profile and be covered more prominently by the press.

Table 7.1 **Insider and outsider pressure groups**

Insiders	Outsiders
Are compatible with government	Are incompatible with government
Are regularly consulted by the decision makers	Are not regularly consulted
Work with the government	Engage in direct action and civil disobedience to put pressure on the decision makers
Have privileged status	Are not seen as having useful expertise or objectivity
Have expert knowledge	Usually campaign on controversial issues

Show your understanding

1 Describe, using examples, some of the key differences between cause and sectional groups.
2 Create a detailed table explaining the advantages and disadvantages of being an insider group and of being an outsider group.
3 In your own words, explain the terms 'ear of the government' and 'behind closed doors' in relation to pressure groups.
4 Why do you think that some groups feel the need to become an outsider group?
5 Why are trade unionists and the Scottish Government against the 2016 Trade Union Bill?

Develop your skills

With a partner, create a detailed presentation on pressure groups with the aim of identifying cause, sectional, insider and outsider features. Use examples to justify your findings.

How influential are pressure groups?

A key debate regarding pressure groups is whether they are influential and/or successful in the UK's democratic system. While most would recognise that they can have influence in decision making, the extent of this influence is heavily dependent upon a number of factors:

- their relationship with the government of the day (as discussed earlier)
- the group aims and context
- the group status and access
- methods
- the group's resources.

Group aims and context

Precisely what a pressure group hopes to achieve is central to assessing their chances of influencing decision making. If their goal is seen as unachievable, open-ended, expensive or global then it becomes harder to recognise their success. For example, the Campaign for Nuclear Disarmament (CND) hopes not only to bring to an end the UK's nuclear deterrent but also to achieve a worldwide Nuclear Weapons Convention that would ban all nuclear weapons. The CND has been campaigning for a number of decades and is likely to continue to do so for decades to come. The CND may argue that it is successful for merely bringing the issue into the public's consciousness but it is unlikely to ever fully achieve their goals in an increasingly complex world.

However, smaller pressure groups with more achievable aims can be fully successful if they gain the change they seek. For example, Tripping Up Trump is a small-scale but influential pressure group that is protesting about the efforts of American businessman Donald Trump to expand his golf resort in the Menie Estate, Aberdeenshire. The group argues that the land deserves to be protected as it is of environmental importance. One way in which the group has been successful is by acquiring land around the site, so restricting Trump's planned expansion.

In addition, groups whose aims enjoy a large measure of support among the broader public and legislators are more likely to be successful. These groups are 'pushing at an open door' and will fare better than those 'swimming against the tide' of public opinion. For example, Jamie Oliver's Feed Me Better campaign was always likely to receive more public backing than the National Association for the Care and Resettlement of Offenders' efforts to rehabilitate and resettle former prisoners.

Lastly, through time, various issues drift in and out of public debate and, if timed correctly, a pressure group can have great success. For example, in the early 1970s, environmental campaign groups such as Friends of the Earth would have struggled to gain influence. However, as the effects of global warming have become more apparent they may find that attitudes towards their aim are more positive and may result in more success.

Group status and access

As mentioned previously, if a pressure group is regarded as an 'insider' group it is more likely to have its demands met by government. The Confederation of British Industry (CBI) is an organisation that represents the interests of thousands of businesses across the United Kingdom. It is often a key stakeholder in the formation of government policies relating to the business sector. Indeed, the group's close relationship with government was reflected at the 2013 and 2014 CBI annual conferences as David Cameron, when he was Prime Minister, was their keynote speaker. During the speech in 2014 he commented that the CBI was 'vital to Britain's future economic success and recovery'. The CBI has claimed success in persuading the Government to stick with the policy of allowing zero-hour contracts as they provide labour market flexibility which supported job creation during the recent post-recession recovery.

Show your understanding

1 Explain briefly the link between a group's aims and success.
2 Using examples create a spider diagram showing the link between aims and success.
3 Explain the term 'stakeholder' in relation to pressure groups and influence.

Methods

The methods that a pressure group may use to promote its cause and/or issue can have a significant effect on its influence. If a pressure group feels that it has strong influence, it will probably be prepared to keep its actions low-key and more conventional; however, if a pressure group feels that it has little influence or that it is simply being ignored by decision makers then it may publically protest in a legal manner – this is known as direct action. This will often set it on a collision course with the government. The more public a pressure group's methods are, the more likely it is to become an outsider group. Pressure groups need to have a cautious approach to protesting publically. If they begin to be disruptive and break laws then they will be using illegal methods and as a result are highly unlikely to be successful.

Republic

Campaign group Republic successfully challenged the UK Government into releasing details about how much access the Prince of Wales has to government decision making. After campaigning for three years to have secret documents released to the public, Republic won a court battle in December 2015 using a 'freedom of information request'. It was revealed that the Prince was sent confidential Cabinet documents for decades giving him access to policy papers normally only reserved for the Queen and a handful of ministers. While Republic were successful in this campaign, their ultimate goal is to have the monarchy replaced with an elected head of state and the adoption of a new republic constitution. They also claim to represent Britain's 10–12 million republicans.

Figure 7.3 'Bairns not Bombs' protest

Group resources

The human resources such as the size of membership and the skills available to the group can be key factors in determining success. In addition, the finances and equipment available to the group can have a huge effect on the impact a group can make. Groups that benefit from a sizeable membership, such as the RSPB

Table 7.2 **Pressure group methods**

Conventional methods	
Petitions	These can be found via the government's official petitions website and other independent petition websites such as change.org and 38degrees.org.uk. Success stories have included the campaign to save BBC 6 Music radio station from closure and the Gurkha Justice Campaign.
Letter-writing campaigns	These are often used by human rights groups such as Amnesty International to put pressure on politicians. Their Write for Rights campaign encourages visitors to their website to write in support of individuals who have had their human rights infringed.
Marches	Well-organised and peaceful marches are often used to build public support. In 2003 a march organised by the Stop the War coalition saw two million people march through London in an attempt to prevent the invasion of Iraq.
Lobbying	This is where groups will set up meetings to try to persuade politicians to join or support their cause. This method was used very successfully by the Gurkha Justice Campaign.
Research	Many groups commission studies and reports to help boost their cause. The Joseph Rowntree Foundation has commissioned many studies on the negative impact of Conservative austerity cuts. In late 2015 it published its *Monitoring Poverty and Social Exclusion* report in which it criticised the government for decreasing the life-chances of young people. In addition, groups can develop this into a legal challenge. The Child Poverty Action Group made numerous legal challenges to the Coalition Government's welfare changes.
Direct action	
Legal stunts	Surfers Against Sewage have attracted media attention by posing for pictures wearing gas masks, and sitting on toilets on the beach.
Blockades/ occupying areas	In the early 2000s oil refineries were blockaded in protest at high fuel taxes, causing fuel shortages. The government has since been reluctant to increase tax on fuel. More recently, in 2012 the immediate area around St Paul's Cathedral in London was used as a camp for nearly two months by anti-austerity protestors. They had initially planned to camp outside the London Stock Exchange to mirror similar protest at Occupy Wall Street in New York City; however, they were moved to St Paul's instead. In Scotland, the 'Bairns Not Bombs' protest in April 2015 blockaded the entrance to Faslane Naval Base near Helensburgh in an attempt to close down the base for the UK's nuclear deterrent. While illegal, the protest was successful in closing down the base for one day.
Violent illegal activity	Student protests against tuition fees in London in 2010 turned violent. Windows were smashed, Prince Charles' motorcade was attacked and more than 50 people were injured. In November 2015 the anti-capitalist Million Mask March organised by a group called Anonymous ended violently with more than 50 arrests for assaults on police officers, their horses and the destruction of a police car. Anonymous has also been accused of making illegal threats and using intimidation tactics.

with more than 1.2 million members, are bound to receive more attention from decision makers and will likely also benefit from greater finances than those with smaller memberships, although increasingly smaller pressure groups are using 'crowdfunding' tools and websites to generate finances for campaigns. In addition, groups that possess the kinds of skills the group needs will have an advantage over others. For example, it is claimed by many commentators that middle-class groups are often successful because they benefit from a well-educated and articulate membership.

Lastly, in recent times celebrity endorsements have seemed to gain influence – not least as they attract coverage from the media. Emma Watson's work promoting gender inequality for HeForShe and also Jamie Oliver's support of the Feed Me Better campaign, which helped to make changes to school food in England and Wales, have helped propel these groups into the

limelight and as a result they are likely to gain the attention of decision makers.

Show your understanding

1 In your own words, explain why pressure groups choose a variety of methods to get their views heard.
2 Create a detailed spider diagram of the different methods used by pressure groups.
3 Choose two conventional actions and two direct actions and for each find new examples that show these in action. For this task you may wish to use the internet.
4 Explain the following:
   a) why celebrity endorsements have been an effective resource to pressure groups.
   b) why a larger membership is likely to gain the attention of government
   c) the link between social class and pressure groups.

Digital democracy

A key feature of pressure group action in the twenty-first century is the growth of digital democracy. This is because a key strength of many pressure groups is that they are able to effectively use social media to spread influence. Digital democracy allows groups to mount campaigns and spread their influence even if they have modest budgets and resources. It also enables people to become more easily involved in political action. Pressure groups can use digital democracy to educate but it also encourages people to express political views and even organise direct action. However, there has been some debate about how effective digital democracy is in influencing decision makers and some accuse those who participate in social media campaigns as doing the bare minimum for a cause (see Slacktivism on page 133).

Prominent pressure groups and other campaign organisations such as 38 Degrees

can organise campaigns efficiently by using the internet. This can involve mass emailing campaigns, lobbying and letter-writing campaigns.

Social media has particularly enabled groups to organise direct action effectively. While 'outsider' pressure groups have regularly used direct action, they now have the tools to organise protests and events at very short notice and with very little financial cost. This has created a situation where quickly organised demonstrations have led to civil disobedience and law breaking as a result of the police not being able to mobilise quickly enough. Pressure group UK Uncut has often used social media to organise events and protests; most famously members took over branches of Starbucks and food store Fortnum & Mason in London, turning them into services, such as nurseries and libraries, that they considered were threatened by these companies' policies on paying tax.

38 Degrees

38 Degrees is a petitions and political action website that claims it is an online community for more than three million ordinary citizens. While not fighting for one particular issue, it backs campaigns that its community deems to be important and puts pressure on the government via petitions and various other campaign methods.

The name 38 Degrees comes from the angle at which a pile of snowflakes becomes an avalanche. According to 38 Degrees it gives individuals 'a chance to join an avalanche of people working together for a better world'. The group claims to have had a huge amount of influence – in 2013 it led a campaign against government plans to allow the use of pesticides that could harm bees. In April of that year the group delivered a petition of 280,000 signatures to Downing Street and thousands of supporters took part in the March of the Beekeepers on Parliament Square. Following this, major selling website eBay banned the selling of these pesticides and the government promised a report on the issue.

In late 2015, 38 Degrees backed a campaign about junior doctor contract changes in England and Wales and delivered a petition signed by more than 75,000 to Downing Street. The group also backed their community to join in the protests that took place with marches and demonstrations. The Government agreed to renegotiate with the doctors over their pay and conditions. However, these negotiations initially broke down, leading to further strike action by the junior doctors. A settlement was reached in May 2016.

Figure 7.4 The junior doctors protest in November 2015

Show your understanding

Using examples, explain in detail the benefits of pressure groups organising their activity via digital democracy.

12-mark question

Evaluate the effectiveness of pressure groups in influencing government decision making. You should refer to Scotland or the United Kingdom or both in your answer.

Are pressure groups good for democracy?

Arguments for

Pressure groups are regarded by many as an important means of maintaining pluralism and thus improving democracy. Pluralism is exercising power in a variety of ways so it is dispersed as widely as possible so that all citizens can be seen as partners, and therefore share in the responsibility for the direction in which the nation is heading.

Dealing as they often do with minority and specialised issues, pressure groups are a vital link between the public and the government. They encourage people to participate in the democratic process regularly, not just every five years when casting votes in general elections. Also, pressure groups are much more accepted as a legitimate avenue for political participation by the general public than political parties. This is evident in the retaining and recruitment of members. For example, the National Trust makes the claim that 'with around four million members, we are proud to have about six times more members than all the political parties put together'.

Pressure groups also play a critical role in publicising issues and in turn educating the public. They can influence public opinion and play a key role in getting all the 'facts out' for the public to scrutinise and hold those with power to account. They therefore can help hold a government to account throughout their time in office by protesting about undesirable government policies, urging action on issues and even enhancing 'traditional' politics by giving evidence to committees in parliament. It could also be argued that they offer a more 'honest' form of politics which, unlike the party system, does not have to consider distracting influences such as career progression, political deals and control of media spin.

Arguments against

However, it could be argued that any pressure on our elected representatives by external and minority interests threatens our whole democratic process. Inequalities also exist between pressure groups. Well-resourced, wealthy and middle-class pressure groups have a fast track to getting their views heard by those in power due to insider status. Increasingly, wealthy groups are hiring the services of specialist lobbying firms in an attempt to improve their chances of influencing those in power, adding weight to the argument that elitist sections of society wield excessive influence over government policies.

The methods that some pressure groups deploy can also challenge their role in a democracy. At times they can be extreme, violent and illegal. While many may argue that this is justified given our right to free speech, in essence when pressure groups go to extremes it can actually result in people's right to free speech being limited by the authorities to ensure public safety. Also, pressure groups tend to focus on one issue to the exclusion of others. They represent only one side of an argument and challenge the government which has a responsibility to look at all aspects of an issue.

Lastly, in our democratic system political parties become elected using democratic means. They have systems in place where they are elected to stand as candidates and then fight elections in a democratic way. However, pressure groups are not bound by any democratic rules. They are accountable only to their members and not a wider electorate. The organisation may not be internally democratic either and its actions may not necessarily reflect all of its members views and wishes. The key argument is that pressure groups lack democratic legitimacy and so should not be imposing their will on a democratically elected government.

Case study: Liberty

Cause group Liberty works to protect basic rights and freedoms. It achieves this through a mixture of peaceful demonstrations, campaigns and legal action. Its former director is well-known human rights lawyer Shami Chakrabarti, who successfully led the group in challenging the New Labour Government of 1997–2010 in their attempts to extend the 28 days detention without charge for suspected terrorists to up to 90 days. Liberty argued that this was against human rights and threatened to challenge these plans through the courts. Liberty would argue that it enhances democracy as it represents disadvantaged groups against the might of powerful government and large corporations. However, it could also be argued that Liberty is one-sided and so has limited a democratically elected government's responsibility to ensure our safety.

Figure 7.5 Shami Chakrabarti

Show your understanding

1. Explain why pressure groups are seen as essential to maintaining democratic pluralism.
2. Read through the arguments for and against pressure groups being good for democracy. What do you consider are the strongest reasons for? Ensure you are detailed in your answer.
3. Outline the key reasons that would be used to argue that pressure groups can damage democracy.

20-mark question

To what extent are pressure groups a threat to democracy? You should refer to Scotland or the United Kingdom or both in your answer

8 The role and influence of the media in politics

(The influence of the media on voting behaviour is discussed in Chapter 4, pages 56–59.)

The media has four main roles to perform within society – to inform, educate, entertain and advertise. These roles take on various forms such as art, film and music, and although often carrying a message will be primarily produced to entertain us. Likewise, television takes on many roles through the production of various genres of programming. Soaps and dramas will entertain, with documentaries and the news educating and informing us. Buying a newspaper or watching the television will provide us with a source of information that will inform and educate us about local, national and international events; in turn this information will help us form opinions and will undoubtedly shape our views on matters such as politics. Indeed, newspapers and news channels also have websites on the internet that many people are now using instead of traditionally buying a print copy of a newspaper or watching the news on TV in the evening. In fact the *Independent* is no longer a printed daily newspaper but is now only available as an online subscription.

The development of new technology and the rise of electronic media are allowing people to access information instantly. Smartphones such as the iPhone let people find out about politics and current affairs in seconds by reading newspaper apps, watching the news or listening to the radio all on their handset (or ever increasingly on a tablet). Furthermore, social media is carving an important role in the media world with more than a billion people accessing sites such as Facebook and Twitter on a daily basis. New media developments have undoubtedly extended the UK's long history of freedom of the press and broadcasting. Owing to the huge popularity of television and its enormous power as a means of mass communication, television must accept the legal restraints and neutrality that the other forms of media can ignore. In short, the media has an important role in both influencing the legislative process and holding the Executive and its members to account for their actions.

Newspapers

Newspapers have traditionally played a huge part in UK politics. However, according to the Audit Bureau of Circulation, figures show that since January 2001, the total circulation of the UK's ten major national newspapers has declined from 12 million copies sold on average each day to a daily average of 6.5 million copies sold in 2016. That's a decline of approximately 40 per cent. If the same number of copies were lost over the following 15 years, the total average daily circulation would be around 1.7 million daily copies.

Despite circulation falling newspapers remain very important to politicians and political parties. They provide a form of opposition to, and scrutiny of, the government. Furthermore, they not only have a megaphone that lets them dominate the public debate, but they also effectively set the political agenda for the other media and more widely in society. With newspapers relentlessly published every day, the drip-drip effect of stories sets the broad political consensus. Newspapers' powerful influence is exemplified by the fact that political parties employ specialists in 'media communications' to make sure the press coverage of their party is as favourable as possible. These spin doctors are not only commonplace in politics today but regarded as essential. In 2015 when Jeremy Corbyn was elected as leader of the Labour Party he endured a torrid first few weeks at the hands of the newspapers. Within a month Corbyn had employed a spin doctor under the job title of 'Director of Communications and Rebuttal'.

As much as newspapers enjoy free press in the UK, newspapers have to be controlled and work within the law. The Press Complaints Commission (PCC) operates a code of practice that ensures the press have a duty to maintain the highest professional standards, although it must be noted that the PCC is a self-regulated body. Generally speaking, newspapers have to take care not to publish inaccurate or misleading information about individuals, groups, companies or political parties. For example, while newspapers are free to be biased towards a political party they must not tell lies or create false news to the detriment of another political party. In recent times questions have been raised about the ethical and moral standards of the British press after a series of complaints and scandals involving high-profile newspapers (see the Leveson Inquiry case study on page 128).

The art of *spin* in politics

With a relentlessly intrusive media (especially newspapers) that focus increasingly on personality issues as well as policy and events, political spin has become incredibly important in twenty-first-century politics. Political spin is defined as the 'deliberate and systematic attempt to shape perceptions, manipulate situations and direct behaviour to achieve a response that furthers the desired intent of the political party'. There is an obvious attraction for political parties to be able to manage news output and public relations. Media specialists, or spin doctors, can put positive 'spin' on negative stories and will have close relationships with journalists to whom they 'leak' certain stories. A spin doctor understands that releasing a major piece of negative news to the media, such as cuts to the police budget, should be done at a certain time or during certain circumstances. For example, there may be a significant national or global event that will most certainly be front page news on a particular day and therefore that day would be referred to as a 'good day to bury bad news'. Ironically, political spinning and spin doctors in particular have a poor public reputation as spinning stories is seen as manipulating the truth. It can be argued that spin doctors fudge transparency in UK politics.

Table 8.1 Daily newspaper circulation from 2013 to 2015 and 2015 election bias.

Newspaper	2013	2014	2015	2015 election bias
The Sun	2,409,811	2,213,659	1,978,702	Conservatives
Daily Mail	1,863,151	1,780,565	1,688,727	Conservatives
Daily Mirror	1,058,346	992,256	992,235	Labour
The Times	399,339	384,304	396,621	Conservatives
The Guardian	204,440	207,958	185,429	Labour
The Independent	76,802	66,576	61,338	Liberal Democrats

Source: Audit Bureau of Circulation

Case study: The Leveson Inquiry

Background

The Leveson Inquiry was a public, judge-led inquiry set up by then Prime Minister David Cameron to examine the culture, practice and ethics of the British press. It was established in the wake of the phone-hacking scandal at the now-defunct *News of the World* tabloid. Employees of the newspaper were accused of engaging in phone hacking and police bribery, and exercising improper influence in the pursuit of stories. Initially it appeared that the paper's phone-hacking activities were limited to celebrities, politicians and members of the British royal family but in July 2011 it was revealed that the phones of murdered schoolgirl Milly Dowler, relatives of deceased British soldiers, and victims of the 2005 London bombings had also been hacked. These shocking revelations led to public outcry and then the inquiry.

Inquiry and outcome

The Leveson Inquiry ran for more than six months and heard from more than 300 witnesses including Rupert Murdoch and victims of phone hacking. Lord Justice Leveson made broad recommendations relating to how the press is regulated. Newspapers are still self-regulated and the government has no power over what they publish; this is important as free press is a key part of any democracy. However, there is now a press standards body created by the industry, with a new code of conduct. Leveson was clear to ensure the regulation was independent and effective. Post-phone-hacking scandal, Leveson's recommendations are supposed to provide the public with confidence that their complaints are seriously dealt with but still ensure the press are protected from interference from the state.

Added Value idea

The debate surrounding press regulation and ethics would make an ideal topic for your assignment.

Newspaper ownership

Another controversial issue surrounding newspapers is their ownership. If the main argument for newspapers is to exercise the democratic right of free speech then conversely this free speech is controlled by a handful of wealthy people who own and dominate the newspaper industry. More than three-quarters of the press is owned by a handful of billionaires with Rupert Murdoch and Lord Rothermere owning more than half between them, including popular titles such as the *Sun*, the *Daily Mail*, *The Times* and the *Metro*. These wealthy individuals are incredibly powerful, with politicians realising that having the support of the *Sun* could help them win an election. However, a vibrant democracy needs its citizens to have access to a broad range of arguments, news, information and opinions. If this information has an agenda controlled by a few, it serves to undermine the democratic nature of our political system.

Murdoch's political influence highlighted as Prime Minister drops round for drinks

In December 2015 Rupert Murdoch welcomed the then Prime Minister David Cameron through the front door of his home to an exclusive party for just a 'few dozen' friends including George Osborne. Four years after the phone hacking scandal, which rocked the media and political establishment, Cameron's appearance at the party was understood to be his first meeting with Murdoch since his re-election in May 2015. After re-election, Cameron met the editors of Murdoch's papers, *The Times* and the *Sun*, and attended parties given by other media moguls such as Lord Rothermere, the owner of the *Daily Mail*. All of these newspapers supported the Tories in the 2015 election.

Murdoch's gathering was the first to be attended by such political bigwigs since the mogul's huge Kensington Palace party in June 2011. Then Labour leader Ed Miliband and many of his shadow team joined Cameron in full public view before the most devastating of revelations about phone hacking emerged. This party, held at night and at home, may have been smaller but it marks Murdoch's return to the centre of power more than almost anything else, the culmination of the process that has seen him regain his position at the top of British life.

Evan Harris, executive director of campaign group Hacked Off, said 'the relationship between politicians and editors/proprietors is too close for the good of the country'. Undoubtedly, the interconnected relationships between media figures and politicians not only highlight the significant influence that the media has but also the blurred lines between democracy and business.

Source: *Adapted from the* Guardian, *December 2015*

Figure 8.1 Rupert Murdoch has been accused of having too much influence over politics in Britain

Television and radio

Although newspapers are considered to be the most politically influential form of media, television is still a powerful medium for decision makers to communicate with the public. This is because TV remains the major source of news consumption with 75 per cent of UK adults saying they rely on television to tell them what's happening. As in 2010, the live televised leaders' debates of 2015 allowed the main parties to reach voters in their own homes. Party leaders are very conscious that a wrong soundbite or a flustered or hesitant moment live on TV can have devastating consequences on their electoral chances. Furthermore, headline stories in television news programmes like the main six and ten o'clock news can put the Executive under intense scrutiny. The same is true with more investigative programmes like *Newsnight*, *Panorama* and *Question Time*, where enormous pressure can be put on the Executive to account for their actions and policies. There have been many occasions where government ministers have floundered under the intense questioning of presenters such as Jeremy Paxman and Andrew Neil.

This is also the case with radio. The *Today* programme on BBC Radio 4 is an early morning news and current affairs programme with almost seven million daily listeners. It provides regular news bulletins, along with serious and often confrontational political interviews and indepth reports. Digital station LBC (Leading Britain's Conversation) has become increasing popular over recent years with numerous high-profile political guests appearing on air to do interviews and phone-ins. Every second Friday on LBC UKIP leader Nigel Farage takes listeners' questions which in turn has led to many controversial statements by him. In 2016, in reply to a caller, Farage stated he would cut £9 billion from the foreign aid budget if he was in charge. Based in London, LBC has welcomed other notable politicians such as Boris Johnson, Tony Blair, Nick Clegg, George Osborne and Alex Salmond into its studio.

Alex Salmond 'shoots from hip' on weekly LBC radio phone-in

Figure 8.2

Alex Salmond MP, the former First Minister, is hosting a weekly phone-in on a London radio station. Mr Salmond hosts a 30-minute talk show on LBC. Billed as 'honest, straight talking … with a bit of fun', the show follows the same format as that of former Deputy Prime Minister Nick Clegg, who had a slot on Thursday mornings until he was voted out of office.

The station also hosts a fortnightly 'Phone Farage' with former UKIP leader Nigel Farage and a monthly phone-in with the Mayor of London. Listeners are able to call, text, email and send Twitter messages to the SNP's foreign affairs spokesman at Westminster, who says he is 'unburdened from office' and aims to 'shoot straight from the hip'. The timing of his slot between 4pm and 4:30pm, soon after Prime Minister's Questions in the House of Commons, means that Mr Salmond is able to provide comment on political events of the day.

LBC managing editor James Rea said: 'Alex Salmond is one of the most outspoken and straight-talking politicians, with indepth knowledge of Westminster and Scottish politics and he is a vital part of our powerful political line-up.'

Source: *Adapted from the* Scotsman, *January 2016*

Show your understanding

1 Explain the main functions of the media.
2 How has technology changed the way we interact with the media?
3 Describe, in detail and with examples, the extent of influence that newspapers have in politics.
4 Explain 'political spin'.
5 a) How are newspapers regulated?
   b) Read the Leveson Inquiry case study and describe what happened in your own words.
6 Explain the controversy over newspaper ownership in the UK. Refer to the newspaper article on Rupert Murdoch.
7 Outline the various ways that TV and radio are important to the political process.

The internet and social media

The internet is now a huge part of everyone's life. Many people would find it unthinkable to go a day without going online on their phone, tablet or computer. The rise in use and popularity of the internet over the last decade can mainly be attributed to the growth of social media sites such as Facebook, Twitter and sites such as YouTube. In 2016, 86 per cent of households in Great Britain (22.5 million) had internet access, up from 57 per cent in 2006. The internet was accessed every day, or almost every day, by 78 per cent of adults (39.3 million) in Great Britain in 2016, compared with 35 per cent (16.2 million) in 2006, when directly comparable records began. Almost all adults aged 16 to 24 (96 per cent) accessed the internet 'on the go', compared with only 29 per cent of those aged 65 years and over. Social networking was used by 61 per cent of adults and of those 79 per cent did so every day or almost every day. Over the last decade use of the internet has more than doubled; therefore politicians must be active online.

Websites

Prime Minister Theresa May has her own website for the purpose of making the government more open and transparent. On the site, the UK Government has published a huge amount of information about how it is running the country. Through the website transparency.number 10.gov.uk, the government sets out the progress being made by each governmental department. For example, any member of the public can visit the site and read about the policy progress of the Department for International Development. Similarly, the Scottish First Minister, Nicola Sturgeon, has her own website dedicated to informing the public about the work her government is doing on behalf of the people of Scotland.

Furthermore, the public use websites to participate in the political process. Through the government's **e-petitions** website, members of the public can create and sign a petition in the hope that other citizens will sign and support it as well. If a petition receives 100,000 signatures it could be debated in the House of Commons. On page 132 is an extract from an e-petition demanding government action on the legalisation of cannabis. The topic was debated in October 2015 after receiving over 220,000 signatures.

The UK Government also gives members of the public the opportunity to provide their views on bills before they are made into law by going online and commenting through the Public Reading initiative. Former Prime Minister David Cameron commented, 'Right now a tiny percentage of the

E-petition: Make the production, sale and use of cannabis legal

This petition asks the Prime Minister and UK Government to consider legalising cannabis. This petition argues that legalising cannabis could bring in £900 million in taxes every year, save £400 million on policing cannabis and create over 10,000 new jobs. A substance that is safer than alcohol, and has many uses, it is believed to have been used by humans for over 4,000 years, before being made illegal in the UK in 1925.

Government response

Substantial scientific evidence shows cannabis is a harmful drug that can damage human health. There are no plans to legalise cannabis as it would not address the harm to individuals and communities.

Source: *Adapted from petition.parliament.uk*

population writes legislation that will apply to 100 per cent of the population. This makes our laws poorer because it shuts out countless people across the country whose expertise could help. And it makes our politics poorer because it increases the sense that parliament is somehow separate from the people rather than subservient to them. Our new public reading stage will improve the level of debate and scrutiny of bills by giving everyone the opportunity to go online and offer their views on any new legislation. That will mean better laws – and more trust in our politics.' (**Source:** cabinetoffice.gov.uk)

As well as official government sites, there are many other popular news websites that the public use to keep informed about politics. The BBC News site is the most popular news site in the UK with more than 15 million weekly visitors. Other websites such as the Huffington Post are becoming more popular and unlike the BBC can be politically biased. Every major newspaper also has an online presence and it is interesting to note that the *Guardian* has more readers online than it does in print.

Social media

Social media did not have the influence over the last two general elections (or the Scottish elections and referendum) that was anticipated or expected (see page 57). Nonetheless, owing to ever-increasing popularity over the last few years, social media has become the most common way for the public to connect with politicians. The vast majority of Britain's 650 MPs are now on Twitter and are using it increasingly often. In total, UK MPs sent almost a million tweets last year and politicians like Nicola Sturgeon have hundreds of thousands of Facebook followers. It has been commented that the level of engagement by politicians on social media has exploded in the last two years and it is now beyond doubt that social media is a critical part of how an MP/MSP communicates with the outside world. In addition, social media has boosted the personal image of many MPs, who have benefited from revealing shades of personality through their 140-character Twitter messages. Tweeting in an informal way about shopping, weekend plans and hobbies reinforces their human side, boosting likability in an era of low trust in politicians. However, a slip-up or poorly worded comment on social media can seriously damage, if not ruin, a political career. In 2014, Labour MP Emily Thornberry was forced to resign from the Shadow Cabinet after being accused of snobbery when she condescendingly tweeted a picture of a house decked out in St George's flags in Rochester during a by-election. Similarly, SNP MP Mhairi Black's Twitter use came back to haunt her during the 2015 General Election campaign when the print media dug up old tweets from her teenage years. Black had sent some controversial tweets as a 16-year-old about drinking and football, which led to some calling for Nicola Sturgeon to deselect her as the SNP candidate for Paisley & Renfrewshire South.

Case study: Twitter – a force for good in politics?

Social media platforms such as Twitter, Facebook and YouTube provide ways to stimulate citizen engagement in political life and drive up what is known as **e-participation** and **social media activism**. Personal communication via social media brings politicians and parties closer to their potential voters. It allows politicians to communicate faster and reach citizens in a more targeted manner and vice versa, without the intermediate role of mass media. Twitter in particular has been responsible for a boom in e-participation. Reactions, feedback, conversations and debates about political events are generated online as well as support and participation for offline events (see pressure groups in Chapter 7). Through Twitter's hashtagging feature, political movements and gestures have gathered momentum through 'trending' and have entered mainstream politics. During the 2015 UK election campaign Twitter was a source of joy for Ed Miliband when a 17-year-old social media activist managed to get huge support for him via her #Milifandom hashtag. According to the hashtag creator, Milifandom aimed to generate online support for Miliband as he was being 'bullied by Rupert Murdoch's newspapers'. Milifandom entered mainstream society and was regularly used by Miliband as a way of improving his often derided image. Other notable hashtags that swelled into online movements include #refugeeswelcome, #marriageequality and #resigncameron in response to former Prime Minister David Cameron's involvement in the Panama Papers furore.

However, Twitter's increasing role in politics has been criticised by many. As with all social media platforms, Twitter allows a degree of anonymity and people have a tendency to say things they would not say in person (see the case of Cybernats on page 21).

Furthermore, as much as those on Twitter may feel they are engaging with the wider world, many people often only follow people they know, they agree with or they respect, so they don't see the world with all its diversity and difference of opinion. They experience political views on Twitter that broadly agree with their own and some in turn attack those who have opposing views. Labour MP and Twitter user Chris Bryant has stated that the abuse MPs receive online and via Twitter in particular could be regarded as 'political extremism'. As much as Twitter may be responsible for a rise in participation, much of this participation is negative. Ultimately, social media has given a new platform for politics and political activism for people in the UK, like it has done with every other industry, whether it is sport, showbiz or news.

Slacktivism

Also known as clicktivism, slacktivism is a term used to refer to acts of minimal personal effort to support an issue or cause. Slacktivism is most commonly associated with actions such as signing online petitions, liking social network statuses or joining cause-related social networking groups. Critics of slacktivism contend these actions are merely for participant gratification because they lack engagement and commitment and fail to produce any tangible effect in terms of promoting a cause. However, others disagree arguing that slacktivism raises awareness, educates and brings people together in support of a good cause or social issue.

ICT task

In groups of three, create a digital presentation to be shown to the class on the merits and demerits of social media activism. Make reference to e-participation, slacktivism and hashtag movements.

Freedom of Information Act

The Freedom of Information Act became law in 2005, making government more open and accessible and also more transparent and accountable. The Act allows any person to request and receive information from a public body, subject to certain exemptions. These public bodies include central government departments and agencies, local councils, the NHS (including health authorities and hospital trusts), the police, and state schools, colleges and universities. These public bodies have to release information unless it is covered by either a qualified or absolute exemption. Qualified exemptions are enforced if it is in the public interest to keep something secret – for example, information that would prejudice the formulation of government policy, the effective conduct of public affairs, national security or international relations. Freedom of information can be a useful tool for the media to obtain factual background material relating to government policy decisions and legislation. It can also be used to hold the Executive and its members to account and shed light on the decision-making process and generate news stories, by revealing material that would otherwise have remained secret. For this reason pressure groups and the media have been active

users of the legislation, as have the general public. For example, it led to details of MPs' expenses being put into the public domain. Details of claims under the second homes allowance used to be kept secret, but Freedom of Information campaigners won a High Court case to get them released after years of battling with the House of Commons. This extra scrutiny tool of the media and pressure groups has resulted in the government fighting back with attempts to discourage its use, at times trying to spoil newspaper scoops by posting replies to requests online, therefore making them available to all journalists, rather than only to those who had taken the trouble to make the request.

Show your understanding

1 Outline statistics to show the rise of internet and social media use.
2 In what ways do websites allow for increased engagement in politics?
3 a) Provide evidence to show the significant increase in social media use by politicians.
  b) Using the Twitter case study, outline some of the positives and negatives of political debate on Twitter. Give examples.
4 What is 'slacktivism'?
5 How can the Freedom of Information Act be used to hold the Executive to account?

12-mark questions

1 Evaluate the influence of the media in holding the government to account.
2 Analyse the ways in which the media can scrutinise the Executive.

9 Assessment

Welcome to the new Curriculum for Excellence (CfE) Higher Modern Studies!

The Higher award is made up of internally and externally graded assessments. To achieve the award you need to pass the internal assessment for each of the following units:

- Democracy in Scotland and the United Kingdom
- Social Issues in the United Kingdom
- International Issues.

The Added Value for CfE Higher Modern Studies is an externally assessed course assessment. This consists of two components:

- question paper
- assignment.

To gain the course award all units and overall course assessment must be passed. The marks awarded for the question paper and the assignment are added together and an overall mark indicates pass or fail. The course award is graded A to D.

The question paper

The question paper is worth a total of 60 marks, with 20 marks awarded for each unit of the course. Essay questions are allocated 44 marks in total and source-based questions 16 marks in total. The duration of the exam is 2 hours and 15 minutes.

Essay questions/extended response

Essay questions are allocated either 12 or 20 marks. Examples of the styles of questions are given below.

Evaluate the effectiveness of parliamentary representatives in holding the Government to account. (**12 marks**)

Analyse the different lifestyle choices that may result in poor health. (**12 marks**)

To what extent are pressure groups effective in influencing government decisions? (**20 marks**)

Electoral systems do not always provide for fair representation. **Discuss**. (**20 marks**)

Source-based questions

These questions are allocated 8 marks and appear in any two of the three sections of the exam. There is no choice of source-based questions – for example, if there is a source-based question in the Democracy section it will either be a United Kingdom or a Scottish question.

There are two types of source-based questions:

1 one that asks 'to what extent' something is accurate or true, and
2 one that asks you to 'draw conclusions' about a topic.

Both of these questions require you to draw on data that is provided in the form of sources, extracting information that is relevant to the question being asked, and to justify your answer using evidence from these sources.

For an example of some source-based questions, have a look at SQA's Past Paper on the (CfE) Higher Modern Studies page of their website: www.sqa.org/sqa/47924.html.

Unit assessment

You will be expected to answer a skills-based question/activity and a knowledge and understanding question/activity. For the internal assessment of the Democracy unit the skills and knowledge that will be assessed are as outlined in outcome 1 and outcome 2.

Outcome 1

Use between two and four sources of information to detect and explain the degree of objectivity in contexts relating to democracy in the Scottish and United Kingdom political systems.

Outcome 2

Draw on factual and theoretical knowledge and understanding of Scottish and United Kingdom political systems to give detailed description, explanations and analysis of a complex political issue.

Assessment evidence

Evidence for successful completion of both outcomes can be based on a range of activities:

- written responses
- slides in support of an oral presentation
- video/audio recording
- candidate's notes used to support an oral presentation.

The assignment

The assignment is worth 30 marks out of a total of 90 marks for the course, and contributes 33 per cent of the total marks for the course. The assignment task is to research a Modern Studies issue with alternative views. You will use your two one-sided A4 sheets (Modern Studies research evidence) to support you in presenting the findings of your research. The duration of the write-up is 1 hour and 30 minutes

The assignment applies research and decision-making skills in the context of a Modern Studies issue. You can choose a political, social or international issue. The information collected should display knowledge and understanding of the topic or issue chosen. SQA recommends that you should devote about 8 hours for the research stage, including preparation time for the production of evidence.

The results of the research will be written up under controlled assessment conditions and must be completed within 1 hour and 30 minutes. Your Modern Studies research evidence recorded on up to two single-sided sheets of A4 will consist of materials collected during the research stage of the assignment. The allocation of marks is based on the following success criteria:

1 Identify and display knowledge and understanding of the issue about which a decision is to be made, including alternative courses of action

You should choose a decision about which there are alternative views, for example:

To recommend or reject the continuation of FPTP as the UK voting system

or

To recommend or reject the setting up of an elected UK second chamber

You should agree an issue to research with your teacher. Best practice is that your assignment should relate to one or more of the issues that you study in your course:

- Democracy in Scotland and the United Kingdom
- Social Issues in the United Kingdom
- International Issues.

Be careful to ensure that your assignment is a Modern Studies issue and not one more relevant to RMPS or Environmental Science.

2 Analysing and synthesising information from a range of sources including use of specified resources

You will research a wide range of sources to widen your knowledge and understanding of the issue and to provide contrasting views on your chosen issue. By linking information from a variety of sources and viewpoints, you will be able to enrich and synthesise the arguments that are developed in your report. Remember it is important to provide balance in your report and to consider the arguments against your final decision/recommendation.

3 Evaluating the usefulness and reliability of a range of sources of information

You will comment on the background and nature of the source. Does it provide only one point of view, are its findings up to date and so are its comments still relevant today?

4 Communicating information using the convention of a report

Remember you are *not* writing an essay. Your report style should include:

- a title
- a formal style that refers to evidence rather than personal opinion
- section headings breaking up the information to present evidence and contrasting arguments in a clear and logical structure
- references to the evidence you have used, especially the research evidence referred to in your A4 sheets
- a statement of the decision you have reached based on the evidence provided.

5 Reaching a decision, supported by evidence about the issue

Your decision should be based on your research evidence and your own background knowledge of the issue.

Possible Democracy titles for your assignment

- Should the House of Lords be replaced by an elected second chamber?
- Should a PR system be used to elect our MPs to the House of Commons?
- Should the United Kingdom introduce a written Constitution?
- Should the voting age be reduced to 16 in UK elections?

Research methods

In Modern Studies we look at a range of political, social and international issues that affect everyone's lives. Many of these issues are based on evidence gathered by research carried out by a whole series of people and organisations – from the government to charities.

Figure 9.1 **Gathering evidence by research**

How do I carry out a piece of research?

When researching a topic in Modern Studies, it is important to consider where you will get your information from. In the twenty-first century, you have access to huge amounts of information at your fingertips on the internet. However, you need to be conscious of its accuracy and the likelihood of it containing bias and exaggeration.

Where do I gather information from?

The information gathered from research can be broken down into two parts – primary information and secondary information – and both will provide qualitative and quantitative information.

Primary information

Primary information is evidence that you have gathered by yourself and is unique to your personal research. The ways in which you gather primary evidence can vary greatly. Here are some examples:

- surveys/questionnaires
- interviews
- emails
- letters
- focus groups
- field studies.

Secondary information

Secondary information is evidence that you have gathered from research carried out by others. You should use it to help support your personal (primary) research. There are vast amounts of secondary information available. Here are just some examples:

- books, newspapers and magazines
- official statistics
- internet search engines and websites
- television and radio programmes
- mobile phone apps
- social media such as Twitter
- library research.

Qualitative and quantitative research

Qualitative research is more focused on how people feel, what their thoughts are and why they make certain choices or decisions. Focus group meetings or one-to-one interviews are typical forms of qualitative research. On the other hand, quantitative research largely uses methods such as questionnaires and surveys with set questions and tick-box answers. It can collate a large amount of data that can be analysed easily and conclusions formulated. Table 9.1 compares both types of research.

Table 9.1 **Qualitative and quantitative research**

	Qualitative research	**Quantitative research**
Objective	To gain an understanding of underlying reasons and motivations To cover prevalent trends in thought and opinion To provide insights into the setting of a problem, generating ideas and/or a hypothesis for later quantitative research	To quantify data and generalise results to the population of interest To measure the incidence of various views and opinions in a chosen sample Sometimes followed by qualitative research which is used to explore some findings further
Sample	Usually a small number of non-representative cases. Respondents selected to fulfil a given quota	Usually a large number of cases representing the population of interest. Randomly selected respondents
Data collection	Unstructured or semi-structured techniques, e.g. individual depth interviews or group discussions	Structured techniques such as online questionnaires, on-street or telephone interviews
Data analysis	Non-statistical	Statistical data is usually in the form of tabulations (tabs). Findings are conclusive and usually descriptive in nature
Outcome	Exploratory and/or investigative. Findings are not conclusive and cannot be used to make generalisations about the population of interest. Develop a sound base for further decision-making	Used to recommend a final course of action

Source: www.snapsurveys.com/qualitative-quantative-research